The Untold
Stories Behind
29 Classic
Logos

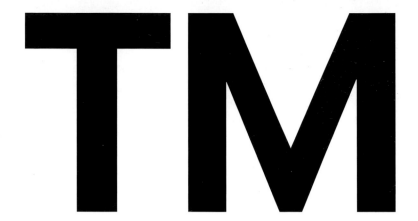

Mark Sinclair

The Untold
Stories Behind
29 Classic
Logos

TM

Mark Sinclair

Contents

Saul Bass
1969

The Bell System was the name given to the sprawling network of 23 separate US companies that provided the country with its telecommunications from the time the first licensed exchanges had been set up in the late 1870s until the group was broken up by the US government in 1984. Headed up by the American Telephone and Telegraph Company (AT&T) from 1885, the system was effectively a sanctioned monopoly. By 1968, it was also the world's biggest corporation with a million employees and 100 million telephone lines running across North America. The scale of the company was unprecedented, and when the designer Saul Bass was asked to look at overhauling the Bell System identity it was the largest design project of its kind.

Bass was by this point one of the best known and most respected designers in the world. He had revolutionized film titles in the late 1950s and, by 1960, had already made his final sequence for director Alfred Hitchcock in the form of a chillingly minimalist piece for *Psycho*. Bass had designed corporate identities and trademarks since the early 1950s, but from the mid-1960s he began working on much more complex programmes for a collection of established American names, such as the aluminium producer Alcoa, Fuller Paints, Hunt-Wesson Foods and the airline Continental.

According to Jennifer Bass and Pat Kirkham's extensive book on Bass's work, in 1968 the Bell System monopoly was already under investigation by the US Department of Justice, while AT&T believed that any sense of an integrated telecoms network was 'undermined by the provision of trademarks and corporate graphics'. Quoting Bass from an article in *Pacific Telephone* magazine in 1970, the book, the designer remarked that his studio's work for Bell would have two goals: 'First, to unify the disparate-looking Bell entities; second, to modernize the look of the corporation. With a more contemporary look, the Bell System might convey what it actually was, a source of state-of-the-art technology and an organization you'd like to work for.'

That the Bell System identity was old-fashioned and stuck in the past ('a mess' Bass later said in the magazine feature) was an opinion reinforced by the 30-minute film created for the pitch for the work. Bass's presentations to clients were legendary, and the amount of work that went into the Bell System film – entitled, simply, *Design* – is astonishing. The visual concept for the new identity is only introduced at the halfway point. Prior to the reveal, the communication problems in the organization are diagnosed with clinical, designerly precision.

Saul Bass's logo proudly displayed on a building facade.

While the film charts a brief history of America's relationship with modern products, the voiceover intones how the Bell company fitted into this evolution of consumerism. 'We looked safe, durable, contemporary, part of the vacuum-tube age,' it cajoles

Above and opposite:
A wide range of item and equipment
designs were created, from letterheads,
packaging, wallpaper and uniforms, to
graphics for a fleet of some 135,000 vehicles
(almost as large as that of the US Army).
At this time Bell served over 80 million
customers in the US.

Pacific
Northwest
Bell

the client. The current problem was that 'we still look as though we were responding to the needs of the past', 'we show up looking non-technological' and, therefore, 'we look set in our ways'. In a neat narrative trick, the film is interrupted occasionally by a dissenting voice – 'aren't you exaggerating?' it asks after these concerns are raised – only to be met with a list of other companies who have changed their look in order to connect their brand with the modern world. Visuals of Chase Manhattan, Westinghouse, Con Edison and RCA identities are given as examples.

The kinds of trademark available to the modern corporation are also listed, such as the monogrammatic form, the logotype form, the symbol logotype form, and the film then makes a play of the fact that the Bell identity has gone through some visual changes of its own over the years. In 1921, the lettering on the bell symbol was simplified, it claims. In 1939 the hook was modified and in 1960 the words were removed from the outer ring device. This clever concession then allows Bass's team to, at last, unveil their own new version. Having looked at all the possible bell forms that could express the most up-to-date qualities, the narrator says that the designers emerged 'finally with a bell that has strength and impact, and, above all, the look of today'.

What follows is one of the most in-depth stagings of a potential brand identity ever created. The new logo is shown working in all manner of scenarios – on buildings, paperwork, vehicles, flags, and uniforms (designed by Bass's wife Elaine) – while the constituent parts of the symbol are thoughtfully deconstructed and explained. At its core it is a clean and contemporary take on the familiar bell shape, devoid of letters or extraneous detail – but there was an extra element in the form of blue and yellow stripes. 'In the contemporary world,

Below and opposite:
An initial set of seven graphics manuals were created in 1969 and then updated every few years to ensure consistent and high-quality graphics as new requirements arose.

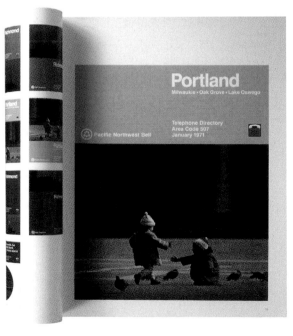

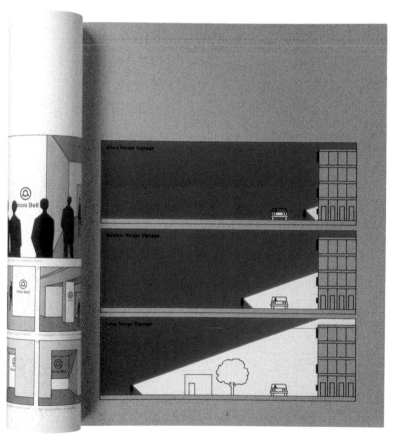

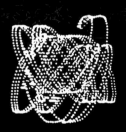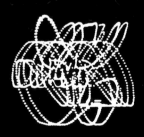

stripes have a message,' runs the voiceover. 'They say competitive, competent, alert, dedicated. They say the things we are.' How could Bell refuse?

The new design was rolled out in 1969. Jennifer Bass and Kirkham make a point of revealing that, 'by the early 1970s the new logo had achieved a remarkable ninety-three percent recognition. More people knew it to be the telephone company logo than knew the name of the president of the United States.' Saul stated, 'they could now run ads signed with just the new bell and the phrase "We Hear You" and everyone understood it was the phone company.'

At the end of the inventive piece of film-making that had first brought Bass's ideas to Bell, it was stressed how 'each impression contributes to the whole, each signal one piece of a mosaic, operated as a national visual communications system'. Bass had transformed an unrelated, disparate and old-fashioned series of company identities into a visually unified and coordinated enterprise. Finally, Bell really was a system.

Fifteen years later, however, under pressure from the Department of Justice, AT&T would divest itself of the Bell companies. As a result, a new identity programme was needed. Bass was given the job, but this time, thanks to a Justice Department stipulation, he had only five months to do it. The result was a blue and white striped device which suggested the speed and connectivity of modern communications.

The pace of change of many of the subsidiary Bell companies, however, was much slower. BellSouth continued to use the logo after the 1984 split until the company merged with AT&T in 2006, the same year that Cincinnati Bell also stopped using the identity. The last to display it, Malheur Bell in Oregon, finally retired the circled bell in 2009, 40 years after Bass and his team had first rolled it out across millions of applications.

1939

1964

1969

1984

Gerry Barney,
Design Research Unit
1964

The arrows of indecision. The barbed wire. The crow's feet. In the 50 years since he drew up one of the UK's most recognizable symbols, designer Gerry Barney has probably heard them all. But he doesn't mind. While the British public were to gradually fall out of love with British Rail as an organization, Barney's classic double arrow logo steadfastly carried on, quietly working away as a simple but remarkably relevant piece of design.

Its workhorse resilience is impressive. It survived British Rail's privatization in 1996, the effective re-nationalization of the railway infrastructure in 2002, and remains the de facto symbol for rail stations across the UK, used over a range of applications from platform signage and tickets to websites and travel apps. In representing two sets of tracks and a stylized set of points, Barney's brief to design something 'timeless' looks to have done its job admirably.

In the early 1960s, British Railways, the nationalized rail network brought about by Clement Attlee's Labour government in 1948, was changing. The aim was to turn it into a modern, streamlined organization, with the help of a radical secret weapon: the corporate identity. Canadian Railways had unveiled a bold 'CN' device in 1960, and this modern approach dispelled any doubts that the British Rail crest could not be brought up to date. Out would go the incumbent heraldic badge with its connotations of the steam age – a red lion in the heraldic *sejant erect* position, grasping a train wheel – and in would come sans-serif typography and a total, unifying identity system.

The story of the British Rail symbol began in 1960 when a 21-year-old Barney successfully applied for a job as a lettering artist at the prestigious Design Research Unit (DRU) in London, and quickly established a close working relationship with the studio's co-founder, Milner Gray. Despite being forty years older than his new employee, Gray seemed to have found a kindred spirit in Barney – he became the first person in the studio permitted to work on the head designer's drawings, and the first to address him directly by his first name.

'I was a lettering artist, I wasn't a designer,' says Barney, who went on to co-found his own design studio, Sedley Place, in 1978. 'The designers at DRU were given the brief and, to my knowledge, it didn't satisfy Milner. So he threw it open to the rest of the studio, six or seven people. I just happened to think of this symbol.' Appropriately enough, Barney first sketched the idea 'on the back of an envelope' while taking the Tube to work. 'When I got to the office I drew it up,' he says. 'It was exactly how I drew it the first time, with straighter lines. I just had to formalize it.'

DRU produced around 50 different symbols, Barney recalls, and taped them up on the studio walls. Gray, along with George Williams, director of industrial design for the railways and the representative from the British

Diagram showing the tapering of the angled bars used in the British Rail symbol.

This page:
British Rail carpets in blue and brown
photographed during the filming of the
British Transport Films production, *A
Corporate Identity*, April 1964.

—

Opposite:
Wine glass and cutlery with the British
Rail logo, 1964.

The
new face
of
British Railways

Behind the many forms in which British Railways appear to the travelling or trading customer stands one national undertaking. So wide is the visible range of activity on today's railways - transport by rail, sea and road, engineering, architecture, catering - that this essential unity tends to become obscured. The new house style, now being introduced by stages, throughout the system, is an expression in modern terms of this unity. Everything seen and used frequently by the public, every station, every sign, every piece of printed matter, will be given an instantly recognisable family likeness.

This folder has been designed for further use as a wall sheet. Each side expresses different themes. The front explains the role and function of the new house style; the reverse gives a selection of the key activities of the modern railway in the sixties, of which that house style is the expression.

Serving the passenger

Passenger comfort and travelling amenities are the top priorities in the new trains of the sixties. Some, like the Glasgow Blue Trains of the Clydeside electric service, have already proved how well good design pays in terms of greatly increased revenue within a relatively short time. Another successful new service, the Midland Pullman, has managed to win back passengers from air travel.

Simple, 'unfussy' outlines, brighter colours, more space and light per passenger, a smoother ride in a vehicle that not only looks clean but is easy to keep clean - these are the main elements in modern British train design. It makes full use of the advantages of modern materials and production techniques.

Trains

The latest experimental train, XP 64, now on trial, incorporates improved bogies for a better ride, better thermal and acoustic insulation, pressure heating and ventilation, improved toilets, bigger and double-glazed windows, better vestibules, better lighting, and wider doors for easy access. The more comfortable seating embodies the results of special research. The thoroughness and detail of the work that went into designing and constructing this train is matched by the detailed market research now being carried out among customers on the train itself.

Stations

A station is far more than a group of buildings where the passenger catches his train, buys a ticket, a meal or a newspaper. It expresses the very nature of rail transport. The new stations, with their functional look, provide for a smooth flow of passengers at all times. Clear signposting, logical arrangement of essential services and spacious interiors match the bold, clean shapes of the external structures. There is the minimum of pretension, the maximum of practical commonsense in architectural terms.

Ships

The corporate identity is being extended to the British Rail fleet of over 100 ships. Here, too, the symbol lends an air of continuing purpose in the combination of the colours of pale grey, blue and flame red. The sea voyage is seen to be what it is - an extension of the rail journey.

Publicity

Posters on all British Rail Stations will use the new symbol against a background of approved colours. Eye-catching and incisive, it will compel attention from a distance.

The time-table is the most important of all railway publications, the most frequently seen and consulted. It will therefore feature the new symbol boldly on the cover. The symbol instantly identifies the time-table as a British Rail publication; the colour distinguishes one from another.

Elements of the Corporate Identity

British Rail

The elements of the family likeness, or corporate identity, which can be used and combined in a variety of ways, are:

1. A new, more purposeful symbol. This replaces the hitherto double sausage introduced nearly twenty years ago.
2. Standard House Colours intended to replace the Regional Colours.
3. A shorter name - British Rail - for publicity use and station signs.
4. A distinctive new letter form of thoroughly modern design, for station name boards, signs, and all printed matter.
5. A new livery for rolling stock.

Buffet
← Buffet

Applications

The two-way track symbol lends itself to applications in all kinds of railway settings.

Shown here are: catering, with a table setting in a restaurant car; and the symbol in repetition on a carpet for use in trains and ships. A manual is being prepared to guide everyone in the correct application of the House Style.

Uniforms of more modern cut and style, to be introduced generally, are all part of the new Corporate Identity for British Railways which is now emerging.

This page, clockwise from top left:
British Rail travel centre photographed
during the filming of *A Corporate Identity*,
April 1964.
—
Station inspector and porter wearing
new British Rail uniform, Waterloo station,
London, photographed during the filming
of the British Transport Films production,
The New Face of British Rail, April 1966. The
uniforms featured a new flash on the cap
badge.
—
The British Rail symbol in use on a current
road sign in London.
—
Invitation to *The New Face of British Railways*
exhibition (1965) as shown in the Design
Research Unit 1942–72 exhibition at the
Cubitt Gallery in London, 2011.

Railways Board's Design Panel, then selected a shortlist
of six designs. This eventually came down to two: a
design consisting of two circles and an arrow by the
studio's Collis Clements, and Barney's symbol. 'Arrows
were in fashion,' he recalls.

But in an interesting twist, Clements's design was leaked
to the press – a risk inherent in using outside help to
make the range of materials required to present a logo –
and was subsequently abandoned. 'Curtain fabrics were
produced, carpets were woven, posters were printed,
and it was all put together in the form of an exhibition,'
says Barney of the proposal stage. 'But when Collis's
design got leaked, it only left one – the one I did.'

On closer inspection, Barney's symbol isn't quite as
straightforward as it first appears, and much of this
can be attributed to his background in hand lettering.
'When you do a line of lettering with the characters the
same height, the "o"s can look too small, so they're
always made a bit bigger,' he explains. 'In the BR
[British Rail] symbol, the lines aren't all the same
thickness: where the angled bars meet the horizontal
ones they will appear thicker at the join, so they actually
widen slightly going out. But that comes from lettering,
where you have to pay attention to the counters; the
spaces that are left, not the thing you're drawing.
They work together.'

Writing of the project in the pages of *Design* magazine
in 1965, Robert Spark reflected on some of the basic
visual elements that DRU created for British Rail: the
symbol, the logotype and a palette of house colours.
These elements would then be applied to every part
of the railway system, from locomotives and rolling
stock, to stations and offices, signposts, posters and
publicity material, uniforms and cutlery. Even by the

Look what you gain when you travel by train

Now: London to Bath, a comfortable 69 minutes

Now: London to Bristol Temple Meads, a smooth 85 minutes

Now: London to Cardiff, a relaxing 105 minutes

Now: London to Swansea, an easy 163 minutes

Pick up a free copy of the pocket timetable

Inter-City 125 makes the going easy

PUBLISHED BY BRITISH RAILWAYS BOARD   4647/477   INDF   PRINTED BY ST. MICHAEL'S PRESS, LONDON ENGLAND

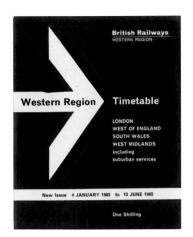

Opposite:
British Rail Inter-City 125 poster, 1977.
—

This page, top to bottom:
A Western Region Timetable, 1965, alludes
to the double arrow design.
—

London Airport Timetable, 1966–67
—

British Rail Timetable, 1984–85, with
inventive use of the symbol rendered in
three dimensions

standards of today's multimedia applications, it was
quite an undertaking.

Barney also recalls a key aspect of the identity design
process that puts a graphic-design myth to bed. Legend
has it that the shortening to 'British Rail' happened
because the DRU simply ran out of time to draw up the
letters for the 'ways' part of the name before the final
pitch took place. However, Barney says that Gray had
planned this change from the start and presented it
as such. 'British Railways were reorganizing the whole
network, making it corporate, so wherever you saw
the name it would appear the same,' he says. 'It was
a nationwide piece of implementation. It couldn't fail,
really, whether you liked it or not.'

At the time, the influence of German and Swiss design
– notable, too, in Jock Kinneir and Margaret Calvert's
Rail Alphabet typeface for the railways – permeated the
Design Research Unit. 'DRU did a packaging concept for
Ilford which looked like Geigy,' says Barney. 'It was a big
change, people were using Helvetica, moving away from
traditional faces. Canadian National seemed to sum it
all up. It was clean. But if you weren't careful – boring. It
took the life and soul out of things. In retrospect, there
was too much, but at the time everyone wanted to use
it; it was exciting.'

One idea of Barney's, which would have rendered the BR
symbol as a supergraphic device, proved to be a bit too
exciting for British Rail. 'The first designs I did for putting
the symbol on a train had it covering practically the
whole engine. It looked bloody great, but they wouldn't
do it,' he recalls.

Following the demise of British Rail, Barney's double
arrow is now a registered trademark in the name of
the Secretary of State for Transport, from whom the
Association of Train Operating Companies can use the
symbol under licence across the UK network. Barney
remains proud of the work, if pleasantly surprised that
it is still in use.

'It worked because it was obvious,' he says. 'When you
think of railways, you think of parallel lines – up this way,
down that way. There was a certain amount of logic I
could use to explain the way it looked, then it was a
question of stylization. I'm proud that it's lasted so long,
more than anything. And I've never thought, "I wish I
could do it again because I'd do it better." I actually
wouldn't know what to do.' Fifty years on, those arrows
seem far from indecisive.

David Gentleman
1969

The designer and artist David Gentleman discussed his admiration for the artisanal marks made by craftsmen, printers and publishers in his book *Artwork*. These symbols, he writes, were emblems of industry that grew out of the workplace, unlike the fanciful winged lions and unicorns of heraldic imagery, which nevertheless still appealed to many British businesses and corporations in the middle of the twentieth century.

Gentleman was asked to design a symbol for Britain's newly nationalized steel industry in 1969. As a supporter of the nationalization policy Gentleman was, he says, 'pleased to do it in the first place', and his belief in the process gave the job 'an extra spur'. At the time, British Steel's director of information services was Will Camp, who had previously been public relations adviser to the Gas Council and had come up with the 'High Speed Gas' slogan during his work there. At British Steel, Camp had already tried to find a symbol for the new organization from several other designers, but nothing had worked. So he approached Gentleman, his London neighbour, for help.

BRITISH STEEL

'Will wanted something in a hurry,' Gentleman recalls. 'It had been going on for a while, he'd been going to good firms for it [and] for whatever reason they hadn't clicked.' Gentleman says he worked on the designs for a symbol for probably not more than a week, maybe a fortnight. 'I was busy on lots of other things.'

He approached the brief very much on his own terms, he says. 'I wanted to do a monochrome symbol that would work with type and in a wide variety of circumstances,' he says, 'and it had to be simple and economical.' Conveying the notion of the steel-making process had occurred to him as a possible hook, and the rolling processes were a starting point for his early ideas, which he executed in Letrafilm, using a compass with a scalpel blade attached to cut clean, circular shapes.

'It started off as simple variants on the letters B and S,' he explains. 'Some contact negatives from my work book from that time show the progress from the initials, and then making play with the counters of these letters, so it became an abstract shape.' His early work on the symbol reveals how he stripped back the two letters almost to the point of negation, taking out as much from the two shapes as possible, only the slightest inference of the initials remaining.

'I was really trying to get it down to bare essentials,' he says. 'It's fairly clear when you see the progression, it's working from first picking out the elements of [the] B and S that would still remind one of what they were, such as the two counters within the B and the shapes within the curves in the S. It gradually developed from that to something involving a roller, a kind of S, the curve curling between a couple of rollers. Once I'd got that idea, I knew it was better than the earlier work; it didn't take me very long to work out the proportions

Illustration of the bent steel bars that would form the two elements of David Gentleman's logo for British Steel

of the positive black parts of the letters and the white spaces that separated them, in 3:2. It just a useful, standard oblong; I didn't want it to be a square.'

The final design also has a geometric purity to it. To create it, Gentleman drew two concentric circles, halved them, and separated and joined them back together via four extended lines, forming a wide S shape from two thick interlocking bars. The S, which had the same proportions as A4, meant it could be easily reproduced at any scale, in positive or negative form.

As reductionist as his formal arrangement ended up being, it remained subject to some artistic feeling. 'If the white line had been too thin, it would have tended to get lost,' says Gentleman, 'but too thick and the black would look feeble. They're all aesthetic considerations.' And while it was designed to appear in both black or white on backgrounds of various colours, the symbol itself could only ever be rendered in one other hue: Pacific Blue (BS0-012).

It was only after finalizing the symbol, having gained an interest in the steel-making process, that Gentleman became aware of the steel 'strips' that were made to show how the metal performed under stress. 'When bent double,' he wrote of these metal samples, 'the best steel wouldn't crack.' His S shape mirrored this act perfectly. The new symbol was then announced 'with all the

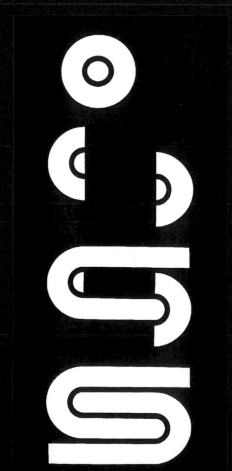

splendour that British Steel could muster," gave the designer. "They had a glossy magazine with a double-page spread about the symbol and my work on it. It was plenty of backing. It was also covered favourably in the press, the wonderful recall about it did encounter from my start when it was shown to executives. If Scan is earning brand for a steel products brand, Steelmag Ltd, which had been trading since 1953 but was sold to The Steelco Corporation in the early 1960s. According to an article in Design magazine, in 1969, ten designers were brought in to resolve the situation, and Gentleman recalls Camp having dealt with the matter. "What he did, I don't know," he says, "they were mollified or comforted in some way to find it was me that I did alter me considerably though. I certainly hadn't been part of any designer dress.

Since British Steel, Gentleman has designed very few other symbols, though he redesigned the original National Trust logo in 1980 and created an identity for Oxford's Bodleian Library in 1999. Two of his most recognizable designs, however, are his blood-spatter graphic for the Stop the War Coalition and the logotype that famously rearranged the letters in the then British Prime Minister's surname as 'Bliar', and was used across posters and banners in protest against the Iraq War. On the portfolio page of his website, alongside People, Buildings, and Wood Engravings, Gentleman also has a section entitled 'Dissent'.

Although the logo for British Steel was in use for 20 years — it went out when the corporation was privatized as Corus in 1989 — Gentleman remains happy with the way his quick work for the organization turned out, and, even at the time, did not tire of seeing it. "I would go to Wales, and there it would be on the top of an enormous gasometer, or you'd see it on vehicles, because of the symbol. Once I was drawing in Northamptonshire, and suddenly, looming out of the fog above me I saw the top of an enormous drag-line excavator, and there was this rib of the crane with British Steel on it hanging down from the sky at me. That was a good moment."

Welcome home

'CBS Television Network'. Soon after, the symbol was simplified as a static device, and the text and cloudy sky that had acted as a background were removed. To add another layer to the story of inspiration, it has been pointed out that this version of the eye device, shown on a background of clouds, bears a certain resemblance to René Magritte's painting *The False Mirror*. Perhaps significantly, this work was purchased by New York's Museum of Modern Art in 1936; Golden had been in the city since the early 1930s, and left Condé Nast for CBS in 1937.

Having been simplified, the eye was then transferred onto rate cards, cameras, curtains, company buildings, even matchboxes and ashtrays. In the lobby of the CBS building, some 3,600 eyes made up a graphic display on one wall, a backdrop that Golden once stood in front of – the epitome of designerly nonchalance – for a publicity photo in 1953. If the company name was used alongside the symbol, it was to be set in what Golden referred to as 'Didot Bodoni', and in 1966, under Dorfsman's direction, a CBS Didot was redrawn by Freeman Craw.

Following on from the eye's debut, preparations for the next season began, so Golden reputedly started work on a new symbol, but Stanton interjected. 'Just when you're beginning to be bored with what you've done is when it's beginning to be noticed by your audience,' he is reported to have said. The symbol's permanence was further implied, Spigel notes, when a large-scale eye device was fixed to the upper corners of CBS Television City building's exterior, 'recalling its similar corner placement in newspaper advertisements and on-air title art.'

CBS has used the eye device ever since, and it currently appears, unaltered since 1951, on no fewer than ten subdivisions of the brand. In 2006 it was placed just above the on-screen show titles of all CBS programmes – the space in which, more commonly, an official trademark device appears.

Below:
CBS advertisement for the trade press, shown here in the *The New York Times,* 13 March 1969.
—
Opposite, top to bottom:
Mock classified ad for CBS which appeared in *Variety* magazine.

Lou Dorfsman's concept rendering for the network's 1976 on-air campaign, the 'sizzle' eye.

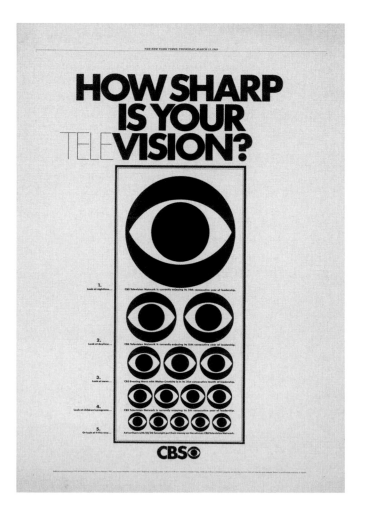

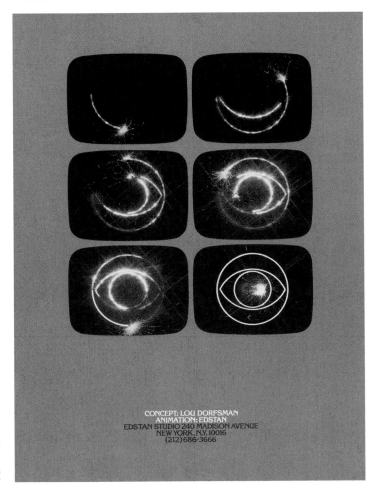

CONCEPT: LOU DORFSMAN
ANIMATION: EDSTAN
EDSTAN STUDIO 240 MADISON AVENUE
NEW YORK, N.Y. 10016
(212) 686-3666

Jean Widmer,
Visuel Design Association
1977

The Centre Georges Pompidou (CGP) is named after the French president who commissioned one of the most radical architectural projects ever constructed in Paris. Known as Beaubourg, after the area in which it resides, the CGP houses the Bpi (Bibliothèque publique d'information) public library, the IRCAM (Institute for Music/Acoustic Research & Coordination) centre and the Musée National d'Art Moderne, the largest collection of modern art in Europe. Yet even visitors who know little about what can be found inside the vast building recognize its distinctive shape – or, rather, its display of its own insides on the outside. The unique construction of the building, which was designed by architects Renzo Piano and Richard Rogers and opened in January 1977, directly influenced the creation of its logo.

Designed by Jean Widmer of Visuel Design Association (VDA, which he founded with Ernst Hiestand), the symbol was one of the last visual elements of the complex to be conceived. It was not even part of Visuel's original commission in 1974, and has, particularly in the run-up to the centre's reopening in 2000, been subjected to rather sporadic use as the Pompidou's own symbolic device. Widmer's own explorations into national Swiss graphic design had initially been brought to Paris through the identity work he created for the Centre de Création Industrielle (CCI), which he had completed, along with a series of striking geometric posters, in 1969.

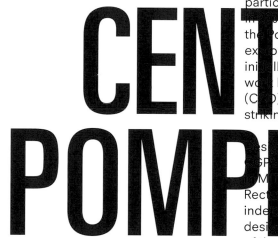

Design historian Catherine de Smet researched the CGP's archives for her case study on Widmer's work in MIT's *Design Issues* journal 'About One Striped Rectangle' and revealed that 20 agencies and independent designers were approached to submit designs for the institution's strategy, as well as details of the resources that would be necessary to achieve their aims. The designers included such renowned figures as Massimo Vignelli, Otl Aicher, Lance Wyman, Alan Fletcher and Theo Crosby, F.H.K. Henrion and Roman Cieslewicz, and the firms Wolff Olins in London and Chermayeff & Geismar in New York.

Quoting from an introductory letter from the Etablissement Public du Centre Beaubourg's president Robert Bordaz, de Smet suggests that 'no design proposal was specifically required, and the visual aspect of the dossier seemed optional: "You may, if you wish, complete this document with an illustration of your conceptions."' De Smet notes that the brief contained two essential elements to address: access to and movement within the centre, and its public image. Of the solutions, Widmer's appeared to be the most expensive, she claims, coming in at just over 1.7m francs.

Widmer's presentation document was an ambitious statement in its own right. It consisted of several sheets of A3 paper tied together so that it could be opened and spread out over a long table, enabling the viewer

Centre Georges Pompidou greetings card featuring an illustration of a crowd of people gathered on the institution's logo.

VDA Visual Design Association

Projekt/projet Centre Beaubourg
Datum/date novembre 74
Seite/page
betrifft/concerne 1er concept d'image de marque
pour le CB

Clockwise from above:
Visuel Design Association's (VDA) accordion-fold presentation document for the signage system for what was then the Centre Beauborg, 1974.
—
Document by VDA showing the institution's signage system and using an image of the distinctive structure of the Centre Pompidou on its cover.
—
VDA's vertical signage for the Musée National d'Art Moderne (in red) and the Bibliothèque publique d'information (green) within the Centre Pompidou.

Top to bottom:
Early sketches of Jean Widmer's logo for the Centre Pompidou, 1976. The logo itself was decided upon in the latter stages of the creation of a signage system for the institution which Widmer and Ernst Hiestand's Visuel Design Association had been involved in since the mid-1970s. When Hiestand left in 1976, the studio became known as Visuel Design.
—
Exterior of the Centre Pompidou, showing the distinctive walkways and escalators, designed by Renzo Piano and Richard Rogers. The institution opened in January 1977.

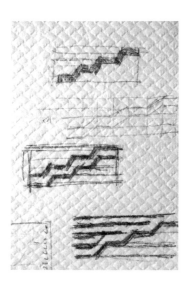

to see the whole campaign at once. Yet among the extensive strategy for signage, there was no logo for the Pompidou itself; Widmer and his colleagues had not proffered one. Indeed, 'although the issue of descriptive signage was the order of the day, converging with the very fashionable trend of "environmental design",' writes de Smet, 'logos were in a state of crisis.'

Visuel Design Association's (VDA) first concept for an actual identity system was essentially a symbol set that would differentiate the CGP's constituent parts – 'a triangle for IRCAM, a circle for CCI, a diamond for the library, and a square for the plastic arts,' de Smet continues – 'all geometric forms that could fit together to constitute a single figure'. This proposal was eventually dropped, however, and more work was done on colour-coding the institution, a programme presented in VDA's Signage Manual of 1976. Lettering, set in a bespoke typewriter face designed by Adrian Frutiger, was placed vertically on signs and printed materials and this, in the first days of the Pompidou's opening in 1977, was the system that visitors encountered.

When it was finally unveiled in 1977, the distinctive striped symbol initially led 'an independent, reserved, and confused existence', says de Smet, and it is odd to consider that 'one of the most successful logos and most striking examples of graphic design in France in

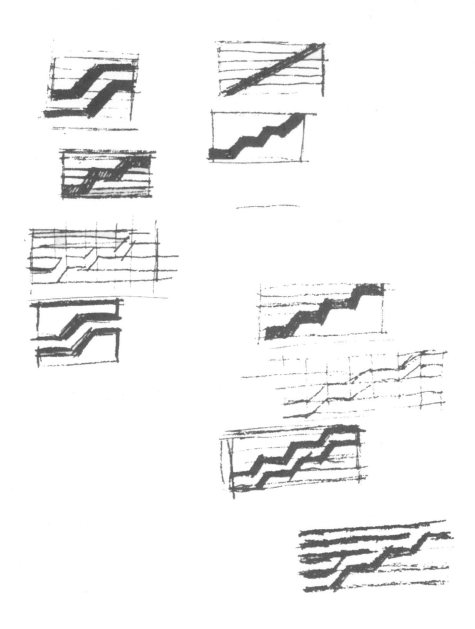

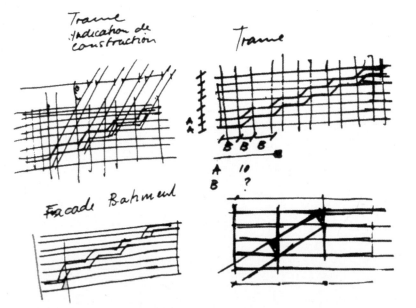

Trame
indication de
construction

Trame

Façade Bâtiment

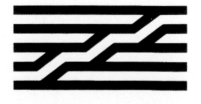

Opposite:
Jean Widmer's initial sketches for the
Centre Pompidou logo, 1976.

—

Below:
Centre Georges Pompidou wordmark and
pages from the logo usage manual, 1977.

Centre
Georges Pompidou

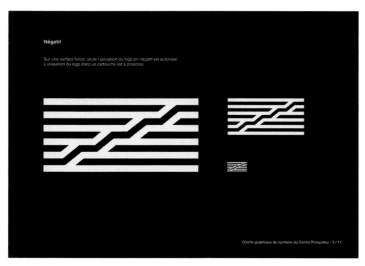

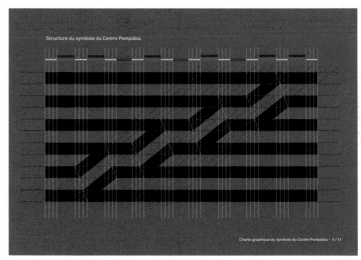

Négatif

Sur une surface foncée, seule l'utilisation du logo en négatif est autorisée.
L'utilisation du logo dans un cartouche est à proscrire.

Charte graphique du symbole du Centre Pompidou - 3 / 11

Structure du symbole du Centre Pompidou

Charte graphique du symbole du Centre Pompidou - 4 / 11

Symbole en outline

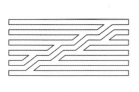

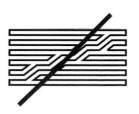

Utilisations proscrites : Détournement

Même intact, le symbole ne peut faire l'objet d'un détournement.

Charte graphique du symbole du Centre Pompidou - 5 / 11

Charte graphique du symbole du Centre Pompidou - 11 / 11

the second half of the twentieth century was produced for the sake of compromise by a designer who thought it superfluous.' Its implementation aside, Widmer's aim with the logo was to distil the architecture of the CGP into a single graphic stamp: eleven stripes signifying the five floors of the building, bisected by a side-on view of the distinctive escalator system that ran along the outside. Like a rectangular flag with an electrical charge running through it, Widmer's simplification of the building alludes to its striking visual appearance, but remains reduced just enough to appear like an abstract, Op Art-like form.

Yet despite its modernity, De Smet notes the similarities with heraldry. 'The two-colour division of the surface into superimposed horizontal bands of the same width, as well as the diagonal band that partially intersects them all, belongs to the geometric vocabulary of coats of arms,' she writes. Moreover, the logo refuses to be a static badge. Rather, it is dynamic, its regular horizontal lines broken by the harsh intrusion of a jagged diagonal. (Widmer has since been known to distort the logo much further in various print incarnations over the years.)

In 1999, however, the Pompidou considered adopting a new identity as part of an extensive renovation programme. But the reaction, from the public and designers alike, was such that Widmer's design was brought back into the fold, aligned further with the CGP typeface, and re-applied by Intégral Ruedi Baur et Associés, the studio commissioned to revamp the identity in time for the millennium.

Alhough it was initially created almost as an afterthought, Widmer's symbol remains one of the most striking logos for a cultural institution. In France, as the designer Philippe Apeloig has noted, it is representative of a break in tradition – a new start. 'By representing the whole building through this pictogram-styled image,' he says, 'it appears almost like a road sign; something that is clear and direct, a signature that represented an abrupt change in the style of communication.'

This page, top to bottom:
Laurens: Le Cubisme 1915–1919
exhibition poster, 1985.
—
System of pictograms VDA designed
for the centre.
—
Opposite:
Posters for various exhibitions at the
Centre Pompidou from, clockwise from
top left, 1986, 1985 and 1989.

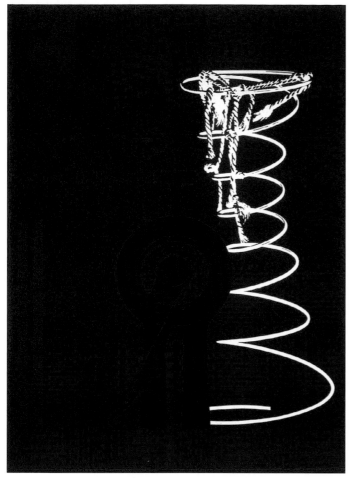

Allan Fleming,
Cooper and Beatty
1960

Media theorist Marshall McLuhan called it 'an icon' and it remains virtually unchanged after more than five decades in use. Allan Fleming's 1960 logo for the Canadian National Railway Company (CN) was created when the designer had just turned 30 and was working at typographic firm, Cooper and Beatty.

In 1959, CN had carried out a survey which revealed that people thought it an 'old-fashioned' and 'backward' organization, hostile to innovation. Dick Wright, CN's head of public relations, commissioned New York designer James Valkus to investigate the problem. Valkus proposed a complete overhaul of CN's visual identity, which would include everything from building exteriors to colour schemes, and a new logo to replace the maple leaf that had been in use since 1943, despite having been reworked in a bright Canadian red in 1954. Valkus gave the job of designing a new logo to Fleming.

During the 1950s, CN had invested nearly $2bn in modernizing its equipment, moving towards computerization and undertaking facility upgrades, with new management and financial structures. The company's public relations team believed that the logo would have to communicate the reality of the new CN. 'At that time, we believed that if CN had a fresh new trademark, people would be more likely to think of it as the technologically advanced, customer-friendly railway it was rapidly becoming,' says Lorne Perry, the former supervisor of CN's visual redesign programme, and later the manager of the corporate identification programme.

Fleming was determined to avoid literal and figurative devices, which would, he believed, age easily. 'A literal drawing in 1944 of an object – even a plant leaf – looks in 1954 as if it was drawn in 1944,' he is reported to have said. 'After five, ten or fifteen years, that symbol would have to be revised. In fact, CN itself has had that history up to now – of constantly revising its trademark bit by bit – and every time it has been revised the one before it is out of date, and it costs a lot of money and a lot of hard work to keep ahead of the game.' There was also a sensible economic consideration here.

After several attempts at the design (which included using a continuous arrow to make a conjoined C and N) the idea came to Fleming when he was on a flight to New York and he sketched it quickly on a napkin. With Valkus, he then worked it up into the future classic. Among Fleming's archive papers, there is a wonderful image of an early version with the following note from Valkus: 'Make thinner & we've got it.'

Having ditched the arrow motif, the continuously flowing line symbolized 'the movement of people, materials, and message from one point to another,' Fleming said. 'The single-thickness stroke is what makes the symbol live. Anything else would lack immediacy and vigour.' Abolishing the R for Railways also made the

CANADIAN NATIONAL

One of Allan Fleming's sketches for the logo for CN, carrying a note from art director Jim Valkus: 'Allan, make thinner & we've got it, Jim.'

Opposite and above:
Allan Fleming with various presentation versions of his CN logo, from a drawing on paper to images of its use on buildings and trains.
—
Left:
Fleming standing in front of CN rolling stock carrying his logo, 1962.

logo bilingual ('Canadien National' as well as 'Canadian National'), an important plus-point in Canada, and made it more suitable for the many non-rail businesses CN ran at the time, such as hotels, telecommunications and ferry services.

The flowing signature logo was a significant departure from the railway heralds of tradition, and was perceived as a risk-taking venture at the time, Perry explains: 'There was a lot of controversy about this bold new look and the CN red, but ultimately the company moved forward with this design because of all the strong features. For the first time, the logo was bilingual and a powerful moving billboard for CN's powerful trains.'

CN unveiled the work in its in-house magazine in January 1961, where it claimed in no uncertain terms that 'our single biggest need is to overcome the notion that we haven't kept pace with the times. No industry can afford to invest a billion dollars in product development without giving some attention to the packaging in which the product is marketed. Visual redesign simply amounts to restyling our package to suit and do justice to the contents.' That same year, the last scheduled CN steam locomotive arrived in Winnipeg, and Fleming's design seemed to fit perfectly with the new age of train travel that was emerging. In 2000, industrial designer Jasper Morrison summed it up as 'a perfect blend of symbol, typography and intent'.

'I think this symbol will last for 50 years at least,' said Fleming of his work. 'I don't think it will need any revision because it is designed with the future in mind. Its very simplicity guarantees its durability.' Fleming was right, it is still going 54 years on.

Opposite:
White-on-red CN logo on the front of a Canadian National train in New Orleans and, below, in Fitzwilliam, British Columbia.
—
This page, clockwise from top left:
Preliminary design sketches for the CN logo by Allan Fleming.
—
Two proposed design concepts by Fleming.
—
The logo as reproduced at small scale – for a model railway set.
—
Christmas card design with CN logo in the shape of candy cane.

Gerald Holtom
1958

The symbol that would become synonymous with the Campaign for Nuclear Disarmament (CND) was first brought to wide public attention on the Easter weekend of 1958 during a march from London to Aldermaston in Berkshire, the site of the Atomic Weapons Research Establishment. The demonstration – the first large-scale anti-nuclear march of its kind – was organized by the Direct Action Committee Against Nuclear War (DAC), one of several smaller groups in the UK that would go on to form CND. Some 500 symbols were held aloft by protesters as they walked the 52 miles from Trafalgar Square, which suggests that the organizers were aware of the need for both political and visual impact.

The fact that, in the form of Gerald Holtom, they already had a professional designer and graduate of the Royal College of Art on board perhaps explains why the symbol achieved immediate success, as well as the swiftness with which it was officially adopted by CND a few months after the march. Holtom was a conscientious objector (during World War II he had worked on a Norfolk farm), and also an established designer. He had created designs as diverse as fabrics based on west African patterns from the late 1930s and a range incorporating photographs of plankton for the Festival of Britain in 1951.

According to Professor Andrew Rigby, writing in *Peace News* in 2012, Holtom was responsible for designing the banners and placards that were to be carried on the Aldermaston march. 'He was convinced that it should have a symbol associated with it that would plant in the public mind a visual image signifying nuclear disarmament,' writes Rigby, 'and which would also convey the theme that it was the responsibility of each and every individual to work to remove the threat of nuclear war.'

In a sense, Holtom's design did represent an individual in pursuit of the cause, albeit in an abstract way. The symbol showed the semaphore for the letters N (both flags held down and angled out from the body) and D (one flag pointing up, the other pointing down), standing for Nuclear Disarmament. But some years later in 1973, when Holtom wrote to Hugh Brock, editor of *Peace News* at the time of the formation of the DAC, the designer gave a different explanation of how he had created the symbol.

'At first he toyed with the idea of using the Christian cross as the dominant motif,' Rigby explains in his article, 'but realized that "in Eastern eyes the Christian Cross was synonymous with crusading tyranny culminating in Belsen and Hiroshima and the manufacture and testing of the H-bomb". He rejected the image of the dove, as it had been appropriated by "the Stalin regime ... to bless and legitimize their H-bomb manufacture".'

Early ceramic badge made by Eric Austin of Kensington CND featuring Gerald Holtom's symbol. The badge was made from white clay with the design painted in negative.

Holtom in fact decided to go for a much more personal approach, as he admitted to Brock. 'I was in despair. Deep despair,' he wrote. 'I drew myself: the representative of an individual in despair, with hands palm outstretched outwards and downwards in the manner of Goya's peasant before the firing squad. I formalized the drawing into a line and put a circle round it. It was ridiculous at first and such a puny thing.'

In Holtom's personal notes, reproduced by peace-symbol historian Ken Kolsbun, the designer recalls then turning the design into a badge. 'I made a drawing of it on a small piece of paper the size of a sixpence and pinned it on to the lapel of my jacket and forgot it,' he wrote. 'In the evening I went to the post office. The girl behind the counter looked at me and said, "What is that badge you are wearing?" I looked down in some surprise and saw the ND symbol pinned on my lapel. I felt rather strange and uneasy wearing a badge. "Oh, that is the new peace symbol," I said. "How interesting, are there many of them?" "No, only one, but I expect there will be quite a lot before long."'

In fact, the first official series of badges made by Eric Austin of the Kensington CND branch were made of white clay with the symbol formed from black paint. According to CND, these were in themselves a symbolic gesture as they were distributed 'with a note explaining that in the event of a nuclear war, these fired pottery badges would be among the few human artifacts to survive the nuclear inferno'.

The symbol itself became more formalized as its usage became more widespread. The earliest pictures of Holtom's design reproduce the submissive 'individual in despair' more clearly: the symbol is constructed of lines that widen out as they meet the circle, where a head,

This page, clockwise from above:
Candles are aligned to form the CND symbol to mark the 50th anniversary of the atomic bomb being dropped on Hiroshima.
—
The original shape of the CND symbol, with widening outstretched 'arms', following Gerald Holtom's design.
—
Students take part in the 1958 London to Aldermaston march.

Opposite:
The rally in Trafalgar Square that marked the culmination of the 1963 march from the Atomic Weapons Establishment in Aldermaston to London.

THE BRITISH PEOPLE ARE
PREPARED TO BE BLOWN TO
ATOMIC DUST IF NECESSARY
Lord Home 1961

This page, top to bottom:
A CND symbol mural at Faslane Peace Camp which was set up at the Faslane Naval Base – the home of Britain's fleet of Trident nuclear-armed submarines.

—

The symbol of CND Cymru (the Welsh Campaign for Nuclear Disarmament) features a daffodil – the national emblem of Wales.

—

Opposite:
The CND symbol has united many different protest groups and causes over the years, from those attending the Don't Attack Iraq demonstration in 2002, led by CND and the Stop the War coalition (top), to those who marched in New York during the Nuclear Non-Proliferation Treaty Review Conference in 2010 (middle). That same year, protesters calling for the withdrawal of troops from Afghanistan also adopted the symbol, using it to striking effect on a series of 'Time to Go' placards (bottom).

feet and outstretched arms might be. But by the early 1960s the lines had thickened and straightened out and designers such as Ken Garland, who worked on CND material from 1962 to 1968, were able to use a bolder incarnation of the symbol in their work. Garland built on the graphic nature of the symbol to create a play of black-and-white shapes for a series of striking posters. He also used a photograph of his daughter Ruth in the design for a leaflet on which the symbol was used in place of the O in 'SAY NO'.

In the UK the symbol has remained the logo of CND since the late 1950s, but internationally it has taken on a broader message signifying peace. For Holtom this perhaps came as a bonus since, according to Rigby, he had been frustrated with his original design, which depicted the struggle inherent in the pursuit of unilateral action. Shortly before the Aldermaston march Holtom experienced what he termed a 'revolution of thought'. He realized, Rigby writes, that if he inverted the symbol 'then it could be seen as representing the tree of life, the tree on which Christ had been crucified and which, for Christians like Gerald Holtom, was a symbol of hope and resurrection. Furthermore, that inverted image of a figure with arms stretched upwards and outwards also represented the semaphore signal for U – Unilateral.'

This last quirk of a symbol that had its message so neatly encapsulated in its design meant it could echo both the frustrations of the anti-nuclear campaigner in the face of political change and the sense of optimism that the task at hand would bring. This was another example of the thinking Holtom would bring to the first march to Aldermaston, which has since become an annual event. Of the lollipop signs he designed for the event, half displayed the symbol in black on white, the other half white on green. 'Just as the church's liturgical colours change over Easter,' CND explain, 'so the colours were to change, "from Winter to Spring, from Death to Life". Black and white would be displayed on Good Friday and Saturday, green and white on Easter Sunday and Monday.'

From the beginning, Holtom's aim had been to help instigate positive change, to bring about a transformation from winter to spring. Today CND continues to pursue this mission, just as the peace movement does internationally.

Delightful Summer and Winter Beverage.

THE IDEAL BRAIN TONIC.

For Headache and Exhaustion.

AT SODA FOUNTAINS.

DRINK
CARBONATED

Coca-Cola

This will cure you if you feel generally miserable or suffer with a thousand and one indescribable bad feelings, both mental and physical, among them low spirits, nervousness, weariness, lifelessness, weakness, dizziness, feeling of fullness, like bloating after eating, or sense of goneness, or blurring of the eyesight, specks floating before the eyes, nervous irritability, gurgling or rumbling sensations in bowels, with heat and nipping pains occasionally, palpitation of heart, short breath on exertion, slow circulation of blood, cold feet, pain and oppression in chest and back, pain around the loins, aching and weariness of the lower limbs, drowsiness after meals, but nervous wakefulness at night, languor in the morning, and a constant feeling of dread, as if something awful was going to happen.

IN BOTTLES 5¢

DO NOT LOSE OR DESTROY THIS BOOK

COPY FOR

ADVERTISING

FROM

The D'Arcy Advertising Co.

Fullerton Building, St. Louis, Mo.

INSTRUCTIONS: Save this book of copy as it will be referred to in our monthly orders, and no other book will be sent unless this is unavoidably lost or destroyed. We will refer to all copy in our monthy order and schedules by **number** only.

Opposite, clockwise from top left:
Magazine advertisement for
Coca-Cola, 1900.
—
Advertisement for bottled Coca-Cola, 1904.
—
Copywriting book from the D'Arcy
Advertising Co.
—
This page, top to bottom:
Straight sided Coca-Cola bottle, 1910.
—
Trademark sheet featuring the slogan
'Drink Coca-Cola', 1970.

Garrett notes Robinson's sense of appropriateness in choosing 'an alliterative compounding of the names of two constituents of the new product'. After one block-letter label appeared with 'kola' changed to 'Cola', the bookkeeper, 'with the flourish of an old-time penman,' Garrett writes, 'polished up his effort by designing, in flowing script, the famous trademark.'

In the late 1880s Pemberton sold a two-thirds stake in the company to George S. Lowndes and Willis E. Venable, the aforementioned soda fountain owner, and Lowndes eventually transferred his share to Woolfolk Walker, formerly of the Pemberton Chemical Company, and Walker's sister, Mrs M.C. Dozier, who had financed the purchase. According to Coca-Cola's history of this period, between 1888 and 1891 the rights to the business were eventually secured by the Atlanta businessman Asa Griggs Candler for a total of around US$2,300 (£1,500), and, over the next few years, Candler was to use his salesman's nous to extend the reach of the brand.

As Coca-Cola's official history puts it, '[Candler] gave away coupons for complimentary first tastes of Coca-Cola, and outfitted distributing pharmacists with clocks, urns, calendars and apothecary scales bearing the Coca-Cola brand.' In this way, the looping Spencerian script became a fixture of many a drugstore. Later, Candler employed Robinson in the venture, and he became secretary of the Coca-Cola Company from 1892 until he retired in 1914, the year he appeared in the case against the Koke Corporation of America. According to company documents from the time, it was at this point that Robinson explained 'he was "practically the originator" of the method of writing the trademark – that it always had the same form from the very beginning. "Some engraver here, by the name of Frank Ridge," he testified, "was brought into it and he and I together worked out that form."'

Given the weight the word 'practically' carries here, perhaps not enough credit has since been given to Ridge, although very little is known about him (a 'Frank Rouse' appears in a story on the evolution of the logo in the July 1978 edition of *Collectibles Monthly* magazine). Robinson clearly claims credit for naming the drink, but did he actually write it out in his bookkeeper's hand? Others have even speculated that the logo could have been drawn up by one of the most famous pen-men of the age, Louis Madarasz. In his book *An Elegant Hand*, William E. Henning considers that while Madarasz could have designed it – his mail-order service was established and well advertised – the finished work displayed little of the expert's finesse.

Henning adds that the link with Madarasz also hinges on the recollection of Warner C. Brownfield, a former student of the master calligrapher, who allegedly told his own student, Del Tysdal, that Madarasz told him he had done it. In any case, it is possible that Robinson's

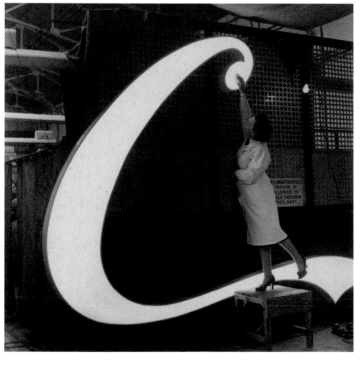

Opposite:
Photographs showing the process of building and installing the Coca-Cola Piccadilly Circus sign in London in 1954. The sign was made by Claude-General Neon Lights Ltd in Wembley, Middlesex, UK.

—

This page, top to bottom:
The finished 'Have a Coke' sign in Piccadilly Circus in 1954.

—

Mechanical drawing of the Piccadilly Circus sign.

① TRADE-MARK IDENTIFICATION

Two forms for showing the product name are essential parts of the designs shown in this Manual:

1. The familiar script trade-mark, famous world-wide and of high recognition value everywhere, is always shown in white on a red background and must appear at least once in every advertisement for Coca-Cola. The basic shape of the background surrounding the script trade-mark is the well-known disc, which is used in nearly all cases where space permits the inclusion of a dominant (reproduction of the) script. An alternate background shape used for the trade-mark in our sign advertising is the squared-oval, or barrel, shape. This shape is used less frequently than the disc, and usually only in instances where it permits a larger, more dominant and more easily recognized script than could be shown in a disc of comparable depth. For this reason, for instance, the barrel shape is used extensively in our stock metal signs.

2. The product name in crisp, contemporary type-style lettering is used in captions and other product lines, similar to the way it is being used in newspaper and magazine advertising to connote modernity. When so shown on painted signs, the product name always appears in red on the white sign background. Coca-Cola in this style lettering must, however, never be used as the sole product identification in a sign. It must always be used in conjunction with the script trade-mark.

Coca-Cola

2

② ALPHABETS FOR HAND-LETTERING

Two new alphabets are being furnished for the lettering of product and dealer (privilege) copy. These alphabets are based on type styles selected especially for readability, simplicity of design and modern appearance. They are very easy to reproduce by hand and should be executed exactly as shown here. Product and dealer alphabets should not be used interchangeably but only as shown in the layouts provided.

ALPHABET FOR PRODUCT COPY

ABCDEFGHIJKLM
NOPQRSTUVWXYZ

abcdefghijklm
nopqrstuvwxyz

.."'!'¯¯^~ ˙:·,¡ $¢*
1234567890 &?!

3

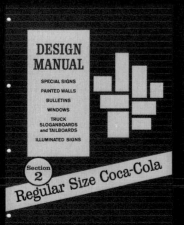

DESIGN MANUAL

SPECIAL SIGNS
PAINTED WALLS
BULLETINS
WINDOWS
TRUCK
SLOGANBOARDS
and TAILBOARDS
ILLUMINATED SIGNS

Section 2
Regular Size Coca-Cola

hesitance to claim full responsibility for the design comes down to the fact that he simply wanted to ensure the man with whom he 'worked out that form' was also properly acknowledged.

Since these early turbulent years, the logo has been the constant presence alongside a wide range of other elements in flux – glass bottles and can designs, packaging, advertising, ever-increasing sub-brands, and so on. Coca-Cola is also sister to a younger trademarked name – Coke – essentially a shorthand version of itself that grew out of the nickname customers coined for the product. If anything, the rise of the name Coke says much about the control that any large brand has (or does not have) over how its audience refers to its products. Here, one name is an elegant, flowing four-syllable run; the other a snappy and blunt command, perfect for using at a soda fountain or in a noisy public bar. One version is as intended by the company, the other as used by the customer.

The trademarking of the Coke name in 1942 repositioned it from being a nickname that Coca-Cola had failed to properly acknowledge in 1905 – when the first of the trademark infringements came about – to being an equal brand name. As the company's advertising of the 1960s was keen to stress, Coke would always mean the same thing as Coca-Cola. Though late to act on trademark issues, this was a keen-eyed move that ensured Coca-Cola owned – and celebrated – its most important derivation.

With the logo set in stone and its shorthand alias now a trademark, the most significant aesthetic change that took place after this time (aside from modish graphic flourishes or stylistic motifs) was the incorporation of the dynamic ribbon underneath the script in 1969. The device was billed as the new look needed to take Coca-Cola into the 1970s. Its effect as an underline seemed to both prove and concede that the lettering of the logo could not be bettered.

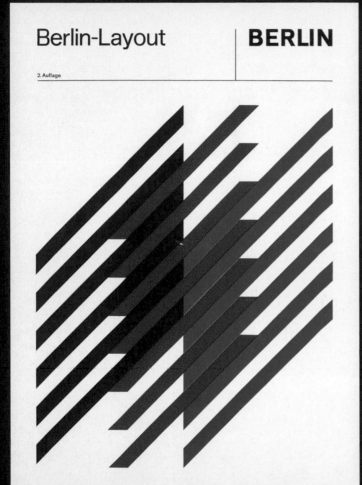

a picture of the 68-year-old Stankowski was captioned with him declaring that 'sometimes it only takes me a second' to come up with a design.

Spiekermann recalls 'the usual public outcry: "That much money for a simple line? My child could have done it", etc.' But there was criticism from designers, too. 'This was the 1970s, there was lots of expressive, US-influenced typography, it was the heyday of ITC in New York,' he says. 'So this clean thing was seen as boring, Teutonic – on-brand, one would say today – and as going back to the 1960s.'

Duschek claimed that the majority of press was positive, however, and the logo soon became one of the most recognizable symbols on West German high streets. He attributed its longevity to the fact that 'it was new, distinctive and timeless'.

With pleasing circularity, Deutsche Bank announced a new brand and visual identity concept in February 2010, as part of which it would employ the symbol on its own, without the accompanying wordmark, just as Stankowski had originally intended all those years ago. The symbol now forms part of a modern brand-identity system which will, the bank claimed, 'meet the needs of today's media convergence where clear iconic symbols are essential'.

When the logo was first introduced Spiekermann took issue with it because 'it was so unemotional and perpetuated an image of Deutsche Bank as being unapproachable and arrogant'. But his opinion changed. 'Now I love it, exactly because it has no meaning,' he says. 'It's just a great painting. But only a brand with as much clout as Deutsche Bank could have pulled it off. It needs repetition and took at least ten years to sink into the public conscience. I bet now its recognition is up there with the Mercedes star.'

ENO

Mike Dempsey,
Carroll, Dempsey & Thirkell
1991

Now approaching its quarter-century, the logo for the English National Opera (ENO) still has the power to surprise those who have not encountered it before. A mark that reflects the broadening audience for classical music, and opera in particular, it is redolent of the ambitions the ENO company had in the early 1990s, and of its attempts to modernize the art form it has championed through challenging and exuberant performances. Designer Mike Dempsey centred his design firmly on 'the voice', and the logo is still singing proudly today.

The genesis of the logo goes back to work that Dempsey, a founder of the Carroll, Dempsey & Thirkell (CDT) studio, had carried out for the newly re-established London Chamber Orchestra (LCO) in 1987. Introduced to the would-be orchestra's lead violinist and conductor at a recording session for some film titles he was working on, Dempsey was told of the plans to resurrect the dormant LCO and asked if he could help with its image.

'I looked at how classical music was being presented at the time, both in print and in performance,' he says. 'It was pretty standard stuff; penguin suits and evening dresses. So I embarked on changing things.' As the orchestra was being put together, Dempsey became involved in all aspects of its presentation, 'from what they wore, how they were lit, the programmes, photography and, importantly, the graphic identity'. Dempsey went on to create the covers of the LCO's ten albums for Virgin Classics, gaining a D&AD silver award for his work in 1989.

The image that had been built up for the LCO had caught the attention of many in the music industry, not least the new marketing director of the English National Opera, Keith Cooper, who had previously been involved in establishing the identity for the Leeds-based Opera North company. CDT were invited in to talk about creating a new identity for the ENO and the following day they got the job. 'At that time ENO had a small in-house studio responsible for all posters and publicity,' says Dempsey. 'The work was erratic and uncoordinated. I spent the early part of my time on the project analysing how design work was produced and the approval process involved.'

The ENO's director general, Peter Jonas, was also open to a new way of thinking, Dempsey recalls. 'At the meeting I told Jonas that in order to do this successfully things would need to change dramatically. The design approval process was lengthy and cumbersome, and everyone seemed to have a view. The main problem area was that individual production directors had right of veto on poster designs. I pointed out that these were mostly freelance creatives who had no particular allegiance to ENO and were more interested in what the poster would look like on their wall, rather than the effectiveness of ENO as an entity in its own right.'

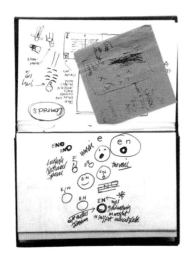

Mike Dempsey's original sketches for the ENO logo, which he worked on during his bus journey to work in London, 1991.

New Production

Eugene
Onegin

Tchaikovsky

March 31
April 7|8|14|16|19|22|27
May 3|6 at 7.30pm
April 30 at 6.00pm

Box Office 071 836 3161

English National Opera
at the London Coliseum

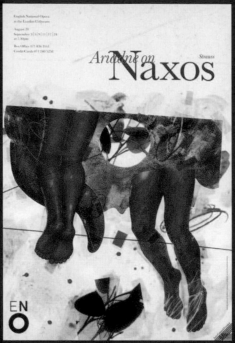

English National Opera
at the London Coliseum

August 26
September 3|5|9|11|17|24
at 7.30pm

Box Office 071 836 3161
Credit Cards 071 240 5258

Ariadne on *Strauss*
Naxos

E N
O

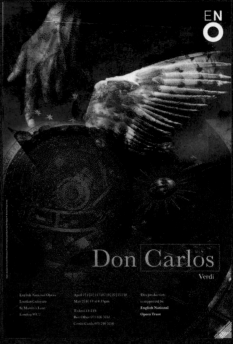

Don Carlos
Verdi

English National Opera   April 27|30|11|14|19|22|25|30
London Coliseum   May 2|8|19 at 6.15pm   This production
St Martin's Lane   is supported by
London WC2   Tickets £4-£49   **English National**
                                Box Office 071 836 3161   **Opera Trust**
                                Credit Cards 071 240 5258

E N
O

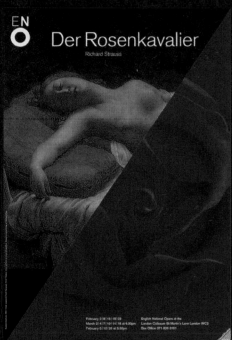

E N
O

Der Rosenkavalier
Richard Strauss

February 2|18|16|18|23   English National Opera at the
March 2|4|7|10|14|16 at 6.30pm London Coliseum St Martin's Lane London WC2
February 8|12|26 at 5.30pm   Box Office 071 836 3161

E N
O

Don

Mozart

English National Opera
at the London Coliseum

October 1|3|6|8|10|13|16|21|23|27|30
November 3|5 at 7.00pm

Box Office 071 836 3161
Credit Cards 071 240 5258

This revival is supported by
English National Opera Trust

E N
O

Verdi

macbeth

May 20|22|28|28   Box Office 071 836 3161   This revival is supported by
June 2|4|8|12|18|24 at 7.30pm   a donation from
Final performance on June 26 (6.30pm) English National Opera   THE MERCERS' COMPANY
in aid of ENO Benevolent Fund   London Coliseum
                            St Martin's Lane
                            London WC2

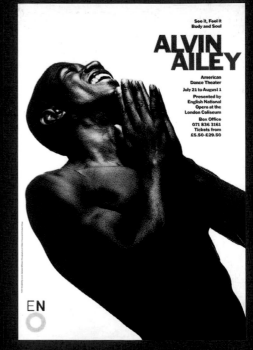

See it, Feel it
Body and Soul

ALVIN AILEY

American
Dance Theater
July 21 to August 1
Presented by
English National
Opera at the
London Coliseum
Box Office
071 836 3161
Tickets from
£5.50–£29.50

EN O

Monteverdi

The Duel of
Tancredi
and Clorinda

in a double bill with

Bluebeard's
Castle

Bartók

March 17 20 23 28 April 2 7 at 7:30pm
Box Office 071 836 3161 Credit Cards 071 240 5258
English National Opera at the London Coliseum
St Martin's Lane London WC2

This double bill is supported
by a donation from
THE BARING FOUNDATION

EN O

HANDEL
XERXES

English National Opera London Coliseum St Martin's Lane London WC2
January 10 16 22 24 29 31 February 5 8 11 14 30 24 March 3 6 at 7:00pm
Box Office 071 836 3161 Credit Cards 071 240 5258

This revival is sponsored by
GUINNESS PLC

Opposite:
ENO logo on display outside the opera
company's home at the London Coliseum.
—
This page, top to bottom:
Stationery designed by Mike Dempsey.
—
Leaflets and booklets art directed by
Dempsey and designed by Fernando
Gutiérrez at Carroll, Dempsey & Thirkell
(CDT), 1991–95.

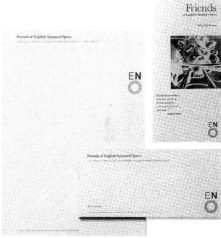

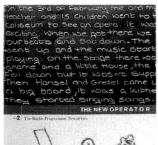

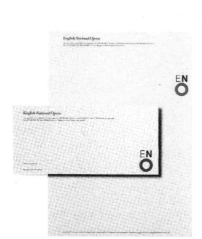

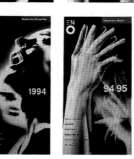

"As a young teenager, my imagination was first set alight in Lilian Baylis's two theatres, Sadler's Wells and The Old Vic. I believe that ENO at the London Coliseum will continue to bring those first formative artistic experiences to the widest audiences of today and tomorrow."

Dennis Marks

Above and right:
Spreads and cover of ENO's Sharing in Success publication, 1993, designed by Mike Dempsey.

—

Opposite, top to bottom:
Truck roof advertisement for ENO, 1991, designed and written by Dempsey.

—

Two posters designed by Dempsey, 1993.

English National Opera

Sharing in Success

According to Dempsey, Jonas digested this reassessment of his opera company and responded with a challenge: if CDT could produce an identity as good as Volkswagen's, then all the issues that the designer had raised would be acted upon.

Inspiration came, as is often the case in London, on public transport. Dempsey took the number 38 bus to work and mulled over design concepts while sitting on the upper deck. 'The ENO project plagued me, mainly because of Jonas's parting comment about VW,' he says. 'I scribbled around with different ideas, but was unhappy. The presentation deadline was looming and still nothing had struck me. Then, while travelling down the Essex Road one morning, I started to think about the very essence of opera. The voice. I started to draw a face with an open mouth. Suddenly I saw it. Two eyes and a large open mouth.'

Much of the resonance of the logo comes from this O seeming to hit a high note. But the eyes are perhaps the subtlest part, intimating being scrunched-up in the act of singing. To achieve the effect, Dempsey used the Akzidenz typeface in two different weights, the E (light) and the N (bold), while the O was drawn as a perfect circle. In doing so he also managed to convey another abstract notion: volume. The ascending thickness of the type worked with the image of the face to create a crescendo effect. 'When first introduced, I also created a complete styling for everything,' says Dempsey who originally brought the Baskerville typeface into all ENO printed material. 'This typographical discipline was incorporated across the board. Originally the O was printed in blue on all stationery items, but on posters and press ads it was always white or black. I have noticed it being used in colour on posters recently. Apart from that it hasn't changed.'

So did he win the challenge set by the director general? 'With great trepidation I unveiled it to Peter Jonas,' Dempsey recalls. 'He looked at it, then at me, smiled and said, "You've done it, that's our VW."'

The project remained with CDT for over a decade, but Jonas left the ENO for the Munich Opera House three years into the campaign. 'After his departure things became a struggle,' says Dempsey. 'The incoming director generals never possessed his understanding or enthusiasm for design, strengthening my belief that a good client is key to creating great work.'

Of the logo, Dempsey believes it is the simplicity of the design that explains its longevity. 'I am pleased that it is still with us,' he says. 'Utter simplicity is often the most difficult thing to achieve, but this is one that I feel I got right and could not improve on.'

ERCO

Otl Aicher
1974

Based in the industrial town of Lüdenscheid in western Germany, ERCO has remained a family-run business dedicated to the creation of light ever since its beginnings in 1934. The company was founded by Arnold Reininghaus, Paul Buschaus and Karl Reeber, and was entered into the Commercial Register on 1 July of that year as Reininghaus & Co. The German pronunciation of 'R. Co.' provided its self-styled acronym.

ERCO emerged into a climate of severe economic depression and high unemployment in a newly formed Nazi Germany. Five years later, war broke out and the manufacturers of industrial lighting focused instead, as many German businesses did at that time, on the war effort. The factory itself was destroyed in an air raid shortly before hostilities ceased.

Rebuilding the company in the post-war climate of reconstruction in the country, Reininghaus and Reeber attempted to reconnect with ERCO customers. Soon enough the brand became the largest manufacturer of 'spring-balance' light fittings in Europe, and gradually the focus of the business moved towards creating lighting systems for buildings. According to one of the company's 13 Basic Principles, ERCO was to consider 'light as the fourth dimension of architecture'.

Klaus-Jürgen Maack, Reininghaus's son-in-law, entered the ERCO management in the mid-1960s and became responsible for product development, market research and, significantly, communication. Maack believed that lifestyle habits in Germany and Europe were changing considerably, and that this, combined with higher incomes and levels of prosperity, would see the emergence of a more discerning market – one that ERCO should respond to.

According to the company, Maack's new vision for ERCO was based on five points, namely that 'light should become the central orientation of the company; product systems should take the place of individual products; findings from lighting technology should be channelled into the development stage; and the design should have a longevity of at least ten years and be the work of renowned designers.' The value that Maack placed on design that could last a long time was then also applied to the look of the company itself.

It was Maack's interest in the set of pictograms created for the 1972 Olympic Games in Munich that first brought him and the designer Otl Aicher together. They met in autumn 1974 to discuss the potential usage rights of the Munich pictograms in a series of back-lit directional signs. According to Maack, writing in 1992 about the issue of ERCO's identity, the designer apparently explained in a few lines what it had taken the company five years to realize: that there was a 'typographic problem', and a lasting solution was sought.

tune the light

The phrase 'tune the light', which alludes to the possibilities of lighting control, became ERCO's tagline in 2006.

This page:
Print material showing the progression
of type sizes in the ERCO logo and the
flow from strong E to light O, 1976. Otl
Aicher employed four different weights
of Univers for the four letters – the O
was drawn up by hand.
—
Opposite, clockwise from top left:
ERCO brochures 'Lighting with LED' (2013)
and 'The Light Factory' (2011). A 2013
catalogue is also shown. These recent
brochures show how the graphic tradition
established by Aicher is still going strong.

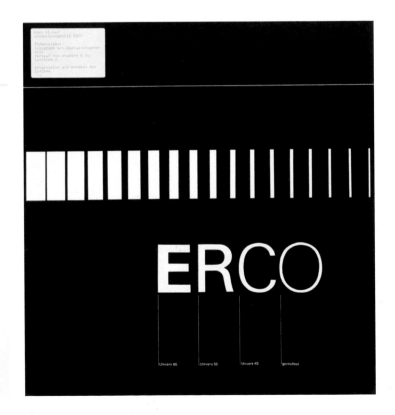

ERCO   Beleuchtung mit LED

Grundlagen
Optoelektronik
Lichtwerkzeuge und Anwendung

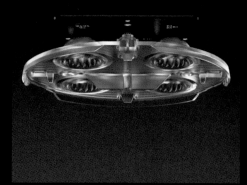

ERCO   Die Lichtfabrik

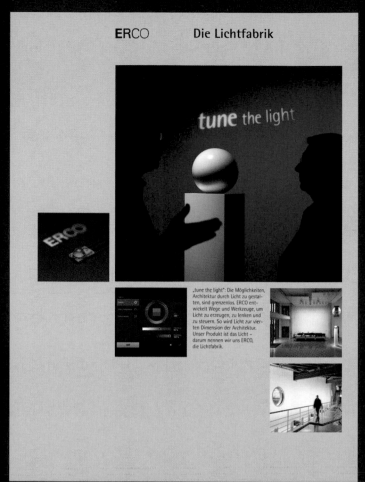

„tune the light": Die Möglichkeiten,
Architektur durch Licht zu gestal-
ten, sind grenzenlos. ERCO ent-
wickelt Wege und Werkzeuge, um
Licht zu erzeugen, zu lenken und
zu steuern. So wird Licht zur vier-
ten Dimension der Architektur.
Unser Produkt ist das Licht –
darum nennen wir uns ERCO,
die Lichtfabrik.

ERCO   Programm

Lichtsteuerung
Innenraum
Außenraum

Ausgabe 2013

100% LED Innovationen
Hochentwickelte LED-Technolo-
gie ist die Basis. Daraus produ-
ziert ERCO mit der ganzen Erfah-
rung der „Lichtfabrik" einfache,
funktionale und praxisgerech-
te Lichtwerkzeuge. Sie erschlie-
ßen effizienten Sehkomfort für
jeden Lichtanwender. 100% LED –
das gilt nicht nur für die Produkt-
neuheiten in diesem Katalog.
100% LED beschreibt auch das
Potential, das ERCO allen Planern
und Nutzern von Licht in der
Architektur eröffnen möchte:
für kreative, nachhaltige und
wirtschaftliche Lichtkonzepte

'The program for the typographical ERCO identity developed methodically,' Maack recalled, 'and began with the redesign of the logotype, spilled over into the design of letterheads, invoice forms, labels, etc.' In 1976 the first corporate brochure was produced, and a graphics manual was also drawn up. Aicher, Maack writes, brought in numerous photographers to show off the ERCO systems in promotional material – a difficult task in itself, since although the products were designed to create light, they were themselves hidden, discreet elements of a building design. According to some, flowers that best reflected the light were specified for the company offices, which proved to be yellow chrysanthemums.

Maack had already discussed with Aicher the discord between the company's then logotype and its typeface, Helvetica. Aicher's idea was to render the logotype in Adrian Frutiger's sans-serif Univers and, later, to introduce a corporate typeface for the business based on his own Rotis family. But the logo itself would prove to be a deft stroke of identity design that encapsulated the ERCO philosophy.

Unusually, Aicher employed four different weights of Univers for each of the four letters. Each is in the 'normal' position according to his numbering system for the typeface (as per the second numeral), with the E rendered in 65 (i.e., medium), the R in 55 (i.e., regular), the C in 45 (i.e., light); and, in order to achieve an even thinner weight than the available ultralight (25) for the last letter, the O was drawn up by hand. It is, essentially, a visual representation of illumination, or rather of the process of moving from darkness to light.

Maack had wanted a long-term approach to ERCO's design, and in hiring Aicher he gained a partnership which continued until Aicher's untimely death in 1991. The brand holds the rights to his pictogram system to this day and in the ERCO logo it also had an identity that would continue to keep up with the pace of technology at the company. And the logo still chimes with two of the ERCO Basic Principles displayed on the company's website: 'Consistently, light is a medium that is not visible but makes things visible' and 'Light has to go along with shadow, semi dark and contrast to make space or objects experiences'.

In just four letters, Aicher had achieved the impossible. He had designed a logo that was also an experience: a logo that lit up and told the story of the very products that the company made.

Opposite:
ERCO print campaigns for products such as: the Zenit – 'Wings direct light', 1995/96 (top); the Quinta – 'A new angle on aiming spotlights', 1992 (bottom left); and the Lucy – 'The new light for your grey matter', 1995/96 (bottom right).
—
Below:
The development of the ERCO logo up until 1976.

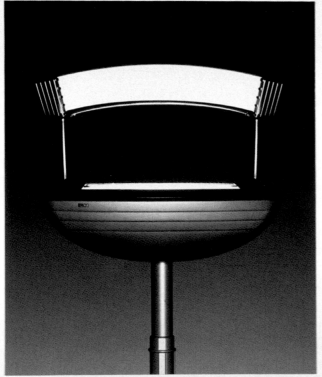

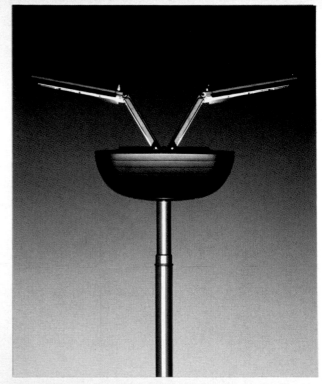

Flügel lenken Licht. Zenit.

Indirekte Allgemeinbeleuchtung steigert das Wohlbefinden. Das allein wäre allerdings noch kein Grund, ein komplett neues Programm aus Stand-, Wand- und Pendelleuchten zu entwickeln.

Mit Zenit gehen wir das Thema indirekte und direkte Beleuchtung differenzierter an. Mit Hilfe von Reflektorflügeln kann ein Teil des Lichtstroms direkt auf Arbeitsflächen gelenkt werden.

Während der andere Teil des Lichts zur Decke geht und dem Raum eine angenehme Indirektbeleuchtung gibt.

Zwei willkommene Effekte der reduzierten Allgemeinbeleuchtung: Die Arbeit am Bildschirm wird nicht durch Reflektionen gestört. Und zur Ergonomie dieser Beleuchtung kommt ihre Wirtschaftlichkeit.

Übrigens, natürlich macht Zenit (Design Knud Holscher)

auch in den eigenen vier Wänden Sinn.

Zenit beflügelt Räume.

ERCO

ERCO

A new angle on aiming spotlights.

A spotlight which can be aimed in various directions is in itself nothing special. A spotlight, however that you can turn in almost any direction, and be sure it will remain there, is rather more interesting. It means that a carefully arranged lighting scene cannot be accidentally or unintentionally changed. The unique means of eliminating such accidents is with the Quinta spotlight range. Two goniometers enable the selected angle to be set with absolute precision.

In form and design, Quinta is significantly reminiscent of the precision and engineering

of a sextant. Created by Danish designer Knud Holscher, Quinta is a synthesis of mechanical function and simplicity of form — a combination which gives Quinta the reliability to remain exactly as set.

Lucy. The new light for your grey matter.

ERCO

What use is a lamp if it either dazzles you or leaves you in the dark when you are working at your computer? When it comes to workplace lighting, new ideas are required. Lucy, a Franco Clivio design, is not

just a new desk lamp, but a precision lighting instrument. It is available for energy-saving compact fluorescent lamps (500 lux), low-voltage tungsten halogen lamps (1000 lux), and incandescent lamps.

Special reflectors and lenses enable you to adjust Lucy precisely to your needs. Whether you are working on computer-generated graphics or simply reading the paper, Lucy is the light for your grey matter.

Glaser used a variation of the typeface American Typewriter for the lettering on the logo. He remains unsure as to why he chose it, 'except for its informality and literary reference, and the fact that it was a rigid counterpoint to the voluptuous heart made it seem appropriate'. Despite the 1970s feel to the typography, Glaser's original design has remained unchanged since its first use, although it has been adopted and reinterpreted by many people keen to capitalize on its association with the city. (According to Glaser, New York State has taken out thousands of copyright infringement claims.)

Designed by Glaser pro bono, I Love New York has become an iconic symbol of New York and is recognized around the world. It is so firmly entrenched in the history, economy and culture of New York State that it is now used as the official logo for New York State Tourism.

Looking back on its longevity, he expresses some surprise. 'No one could have had any idea how significant the logo would become, certainly not me,' he says. 'It's amazing to me that it hasn't vanished, that it is still impactful, that people still respond to it, and it still seems to do its basic job. Perhaps the most remarkable thing about it is not its origins, but its persistence.'

I ❤ NY MORE THAN EVER

BE GENEROUS. YOUR CITY NEEDS YOU. THIS POSTER IS NOT FOR SALE.

Milton Glaser's reinterpretation of his celebrated 1975 poster reflecting last week's terrorist attack on the World Trade Center.

HERMES *for* SPEED   EROS *for* PLEASURE   CHRONOS *for* PUNCTUALITY

CHARON *for* CHEAPNESS   PAN *for the* COUNTRYSIDE

PALLAS *for* SAFETY   PLUTO *for* *travellers* *in the* UNDERGROUND

ALL FIND THEIR HIGHEST AIM IN THE UNDERGROUND

ECLIPSE OF THE SUN
WEDNESDAY, 17th APRIL.
MID TIME 12.10 p.m.

NEAREST STATION.

Primrose Hill	—	Chalk Farm
Parliament Hill	—	Kentish Town
Harrow Hill	—	South Harrow
Horsenden Hill	—	Sudbury Town
Richmond Hill	—	Richmond
Hampstead Hill	—	Hampstead
Golders Hill	—	Golders Green
Wimbledon Hill	—	Wimbledon

NOTHING CAN CAST A SHADOW OVER THE UNDERGROUND

a *fait accompli*,' says Ovenden in his book, *London Underground by Design*. But Sharland's artwork is the only one that can be precisely dated. In 1912, the artist was commissioned by UERL to make a poster promoting the fact that the Underground would be serving the various vantage points across the capital from which the public could watch the solar eclipse on 17 April. His design positioned the 'UndergrounD' logotype on a red disc, which he placed over an image of the moon, with the sun behind forming a ring instead of a solid red disc. (Sharland also created two *Whitsuntide* posters in May 1912 and 1913 that played on the device.)

This bar and ring composition effectively took the hybrid symbol a stage further towards the roundel to which Johnston was commissioned to wed his newly completed Johnston typeface in 1916. The symbol was trademarked in 1917, appeared on map covers in June 1919, and was refined once again in 1920 so that just the U and D appeared over the edge of the ring. By the mid 1920s, Johnston had also produced a set of guidelines for the roundel's reproduction, and the proportions of the bullseye were altered to incorporate the now standardized Johnston face.

1912 was also a key year because of another set of circumstances that may have influenced the roundel's meandering evolutionary path. The joining of Underground services with the London General Omnibus Company (LGOC) that year brought about a symbol that combined the LGOC's 'winged wheel', registered as a trademark in 1905 and used on buses and uniforms, with the Underground's new bar and circle device. This was then used on maps issued by the integrated company, which featured 'General' across the bar and 'Map & Guide' on the ring section.

Once the roundel had been established, Charles Holden became the next significant figure to render the logo in a meaningful way, this time as a vital element in his building designs for several of the stations on the network. According to the London Transport Museum's (LTM) history of the roundel, from the mid-1920s 'Venetian masts appeared outside stations,

This page, top to bottom:
A LGOC double-decker motor bus photographed in 1906 and displaying the 'winged wheel' roundel symbol, which was introduced in 1905.
—
Edward Johnston's drawing of the dimensions for the roundel design, 1919 (left) and the exterior of Temple station (right) showing the entrance canopy and an old-style roundel, 1980.

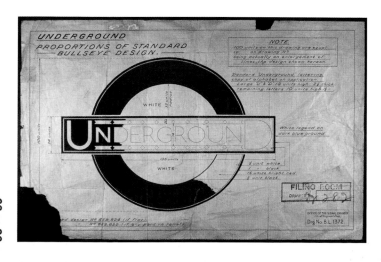

which acted like flagpoles to support the logo in three dimensions. Stained glass roundels were incorporated into clerestory windows above station entrances. The architectural roundel greatly assisted passengers in identifying stations at street level.'

In the early 1930s, Holden began designing stations for the northern and western extensions of the Piccadilly line, which placed roundels in thin bronze frames to match the new handrails and poster frames. 'The roundel which continued to act as a platform name board, was now incorporated into the very fabric of the station interior,' says the LTM. 'During the 1930s, Holden also employed the roundel in his designs for bus stop flags and shelters.'

The birth of London Transport as a trading name for the London Passenger Transport Board, the single authority which in 1933 ran the bus, tram and underground rail services across the city, coincided with a short-lived attempt to replace the roundel. C.W. Bacon was commissioned to design a winged symbol based on the London Passenger Transport Board's initials, but it lasted only a few months, and Pick recommended a return to the roundel device, which Johnston reworked once more to incorporate the London Transport name. The graphic designer Hans Schleger was commissioned in 1935 to redesign the London bus stop, and he retained the colour coding of the various operating services (Green Line coaches, green country buses and red central buses), and created a silhouetted device of the bar and circle. Three years later, in an attempt to make station signage consistent, the first illustrated sign manual was compiled, based on the Carr-Edwards Report on the standardization of signs. The manual, which included guidelines for roundel usage in ticket offices and platforms, essentially formalized the principles developed over previous years and, where relevant, designs that Holden had developed as part of station architecture.

Developing alongside the roundel itself was a legion of posters, each of which referenced the symbol, often in highly creative ways (not least France and Sharland's

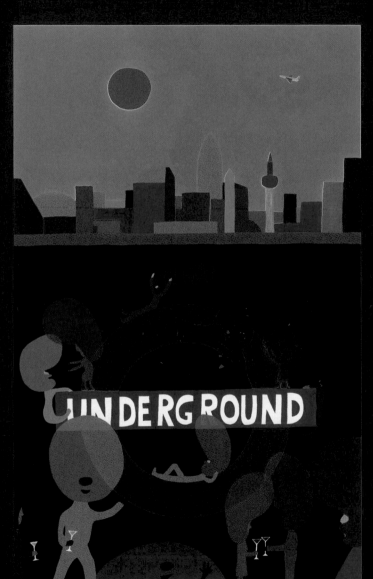

efforts from 1912). For many artists and designers, the symbol acted as a jumping-off point for their work. It was the source of an extending arm thrusting a lever forward in Edward McKnight Kauffer's *Power – The Nerve Centre of London's Underground* poster of 1931 and, in perhaps its most famous incarnation, it was depicted as a planet by the leading Surrealist artist and photographer Man Ray, whose diptych poster, *London Transport – Keeps London Going* (1938), celebrated the symbol as a three-dimensional form.

In the late 1940s, the *At London's Service* poster by Misha Black and John Barker showed a beam of light surveying the city (from one of Ray's planetary roundels), while Abram Games made a yellow version of the symbol into a bowing serviceman. Tom Eckersley saw the bar of the roundel as a pair of directing arms in 1959; while in Games's last poster for London Underground in 1976, it was incorporated into a striking design of a tiger advertising London Zoo.

As a corporate rather than creative device, the Design Research Unit introduced a blue and red roundel from 1972, which was then adapted by Henrion, Ludlow and Schmidt in 1984. Wolff Olins then developed a series of roundels for the other operating subsidiaries of London Regional Transport in 1987 and, since then, the family of roundels has grown to incorporate all the services that Transport for London (formed in 2000) now offers. In 1994, when bus services were privatized and operated on behalf of London Transport, a white roundel on a red square became the main symbol for the bus network; in 2003, London Underground became part of Transport for London and from 2007 part of the suburban rail network was branded as Overground and transferred to the organization, sporting a solid orange bar and circle. While the roundel symbolizes London to many around the world, its influence on international transport systems has also been considerable. The Shanghai Metro, Osaka Municipal Subway and Utah Transit Authority have each adopted a roundel-like device, for example.

Despite its use over an increasing number of applications, the roundel remains a distinctive mark that has, over the course of a century, given itself up to interpretation by artists and designers alike. In 2008 the Art on the Underground organisation launched the Roundel project and commissioned 100 artists to reinterpret the logo in an individual artwork, from which an exhibition, auction and book were to follow. It is certainly rare that such a definitive yet fundamentally simple symbol, where just a bar and a circle can represent a journey across and around London, is able to trigger the imagination to such a degree. In a sense, it is both the roundel's dependable consistency and its determinedly unfixed nature that make it such an appropriate symbol for the city and all it has to offer.

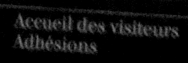
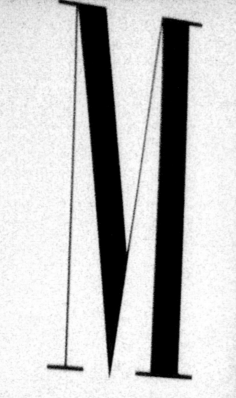

proposals that showed a work of art, the director rejected all the proposals showing the building), Monguzzi was again asked to address the problem and provide a concept. 'The conclusion at the meeting was that just two elements really needed to be on the poster – the logo and the date,' he recalls. 'The logo was already well known, it had been widely used and many articles were in the newspapers talking about this impending birth. In fact, the poster was only reiterating something already known – I was just astounded by the radicalism of the new brief.'

But after numerous attempts Monguzzi felt that a purely typographic approach could not properly evoke a birth. 'Nothing was really starting, nothing was beginning, nothing was taking off,' he says. 'I walked over to my photography books, picked up a Jacques Henri Lartigue album, and slowly began to flip through the pages. [The early work of Lartigue was a perfect fit time-wise, and Lartigue was French]. When I finally came to the image of the glider I stopped. I knew this was the answer.' Monguzzi had settled on Lartigue's 1908 photograph *My Brother, Zissou, Gets His Glider Airborne*. It was the perfect take-off metaphor.

For the poster, Monguzzi incorporated the left half of the image only and completely cut off the bottom third. He needed to turn the image into a symbol. 'When I got back to Paris with this proposal I knew that I had totally disobeyed the brief,' he says. 'But I was confident that they would understand – the image was not shown as a piece of art.' After some deliberation, the museum approved the poster, but there remained a further hurdle.

Lartigue was 92 and the year before had donated his archive to the French state. The Lartigue Foundation had rules in place concerning the use of his work and, in particular, cropping images was not allowed. Monguzzi suggested showing the project to the Foundation anyway. 'When they saw the posters, not only were the rights to use the image as I had planned allowed, but a vintage print of that shot was donated to the Musée d'Orsay photographic collection,' Monguzzi recalls.

A few days after the museum received the approval, on 12 September 1986, Lartigue died. 'The poster became a posthumous homage,' says Monguzzi. 'Three months later, after the museum's opening, Florette Lartigue wrote a touching letter to Jacques Rigaud, the Musée d'Orsay's president, saying how happy her husband would have been in seeing his glider flying all over the roofs of Paris.'

Musée d'Orsay, l'Album souvenir

9 décembre 1986

Opposite, top to bottom:
Museum floor plans (top) and signage
system (below) created by Monguzzi and
Jean Widmer of Visuel Design.

—

A square version of the museum's logo,
in white out of black, was created to sit
alongside the monogram of the Réunion
des Musées Nationaux.

—

Cover of the museum's souvenir
publication, which was available at
the opening.

—

Above:
The poster that Monguzzi designed
announcing the opening of the museum
featured a cropped version of his logo,
the date of the event and an image of a
glider taking off. This came from the 1908
photograph by Jacques Henri Lartigue, a
vintage print of which was subsequently
donated to the museum.

it was clean, progressive, could be read from a mile away, and was easy to use in all mediums.'

In three zooming lines of the same width, Blackburn's minimalist design alluded to the motion and thrill of space exploration. While the crossbar-less As formed the bases of two rockets pointing skyward the N and the S were remarkably similar forms, as if the N could be flipped, put on its side and given a series of right-angled turns to make the S. Fletcher caught something of the sense of balance in the design when he later wrote how it was 'pleasing to the eye and gives a feeling of unity, technological precision, thrust and orientation toward the future'.

While this new rust-coloured logo created a discernable buzz in the room, says Danne, it was also accompanied by a series of illustrations which showed how the studio envisaged the logo being used across a wide range of applications. Presented to the assembled NASA party it was, says Danne, 'a coordinated, comprehensive design programme; not just another ornamental badge to be stuck on a multitude of different products'.

The pitch was successful, and Jim Dean, the studio's contract coordinator at the Agency, called the studio with the good news: 'It's a go!' But the news of the redesign was not communicated to NASA staff with the same efficacy. In fact, Danne suggests, the mishandling of the logo's introduction played a significant role in building up a level of resistance to it. At the time, NASA was essentially a coalition of different Agency Centers that had been operating independently for decades (formerly known as NACA, the Agency had been rebuilt and renamed as NASA on 29 July 1958 by President Eisenhower).

'The Agency made the decision to alert the various Centers to the new Program by sending Executive stationery to each Center Director,' Danne writes. 'That stationery displayed the new NASA Logotype and it would be the first time they were informed of the graphics program and image change. These Centers were like fiefdoms, they enjoyed their freedom and their provincial specialties. At the time of our redesign, there was resistance to almost anything emitting from Headquarters.' This was the environment Danne & Blackburn confronted. Letterheaded 'gifts' from Washington, proudly sporting the new logotype, 'proceeded to detonate across the country ... and all hell broke loose! Our firm wasn't keen on introducing the whole Program in such a shallow and casual way,' says Danne. 'For one thing, the letterhead couldn't explain how thorough and solid the new Graphic System was.' The solution was an arduous studio tour across the US, complete with a PR rep from NASA headquarters in tow, to give the full design presentation to each and every centre.

Below:
Danne & Blackburn's design programme included a graphic standards manual (pages shown, opposite) for NASA which defined everything from signage, aircraft and space vehicle markings (above), to publications, uniforms and film and television titles.
—
Opposite:
Graphic standards manual design by Richard Danne, Bruce Blackburn, Stephen Loges and others.

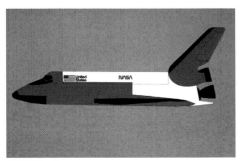

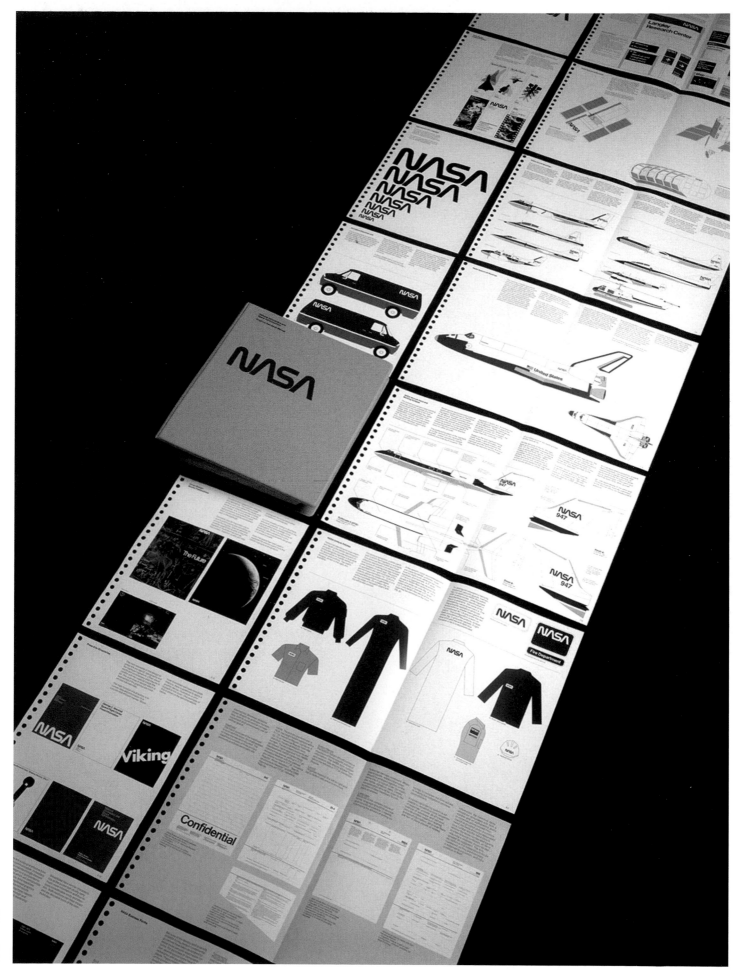

NASA

The Future

On
the
possibility
of
extraterrestrial
life

NASA

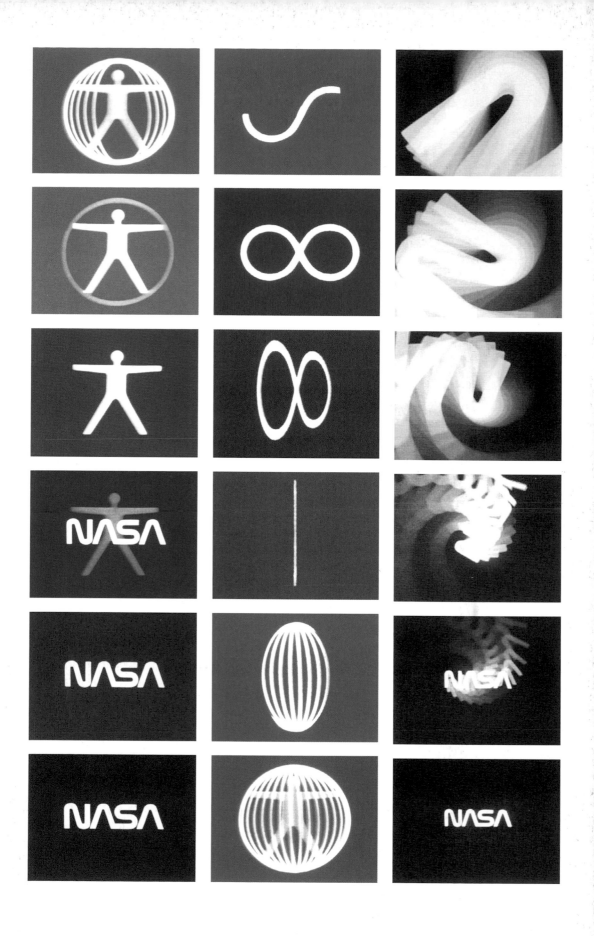

NT

Middleton & Rowley **A Fair Quarrel**

THE CHERRY ORCHARD

by Anton Chekhov translated by **Michael Frayn**

NT
NATIONAL
THEATRE

Judi Bowker
Norman Claridge
Edna Doré
Albert Finney
Susan Fleetwood
Irene Gorst
Nicky Henson
Tamara Hinchco
Martin Howells

Brian Kent
Ben Kingsley
Susan Littler
Marianne Morley
Peter Needham
Richard Perkins
Ralph Richardson
Terence Rigby
Peter Rocca

Helen Ryan
Keith Skinner
Robert Stephens
Derek Thompson
Daniel Thorndike
Dorothy Tutin
Dennis Tynsley
Janet Whiteside

Director
Peter Hall

Designer
John Bury

Lighting
David Hersey

Music
Harrison Birtwistle
and Dominic Muldowney

Dance
Sally Gilpin

Above and opposite:
Posters designed by Richard Bird and
Michael Mayhew for Thomas Middleton
and William Rowley's *A Fair Quarrel*, 1979;
Chekhov's *The Cherry Orchard*, 1978; and
Ben Jonson's *Volpone or The Fox*, 1977
(illustrator uncredited).

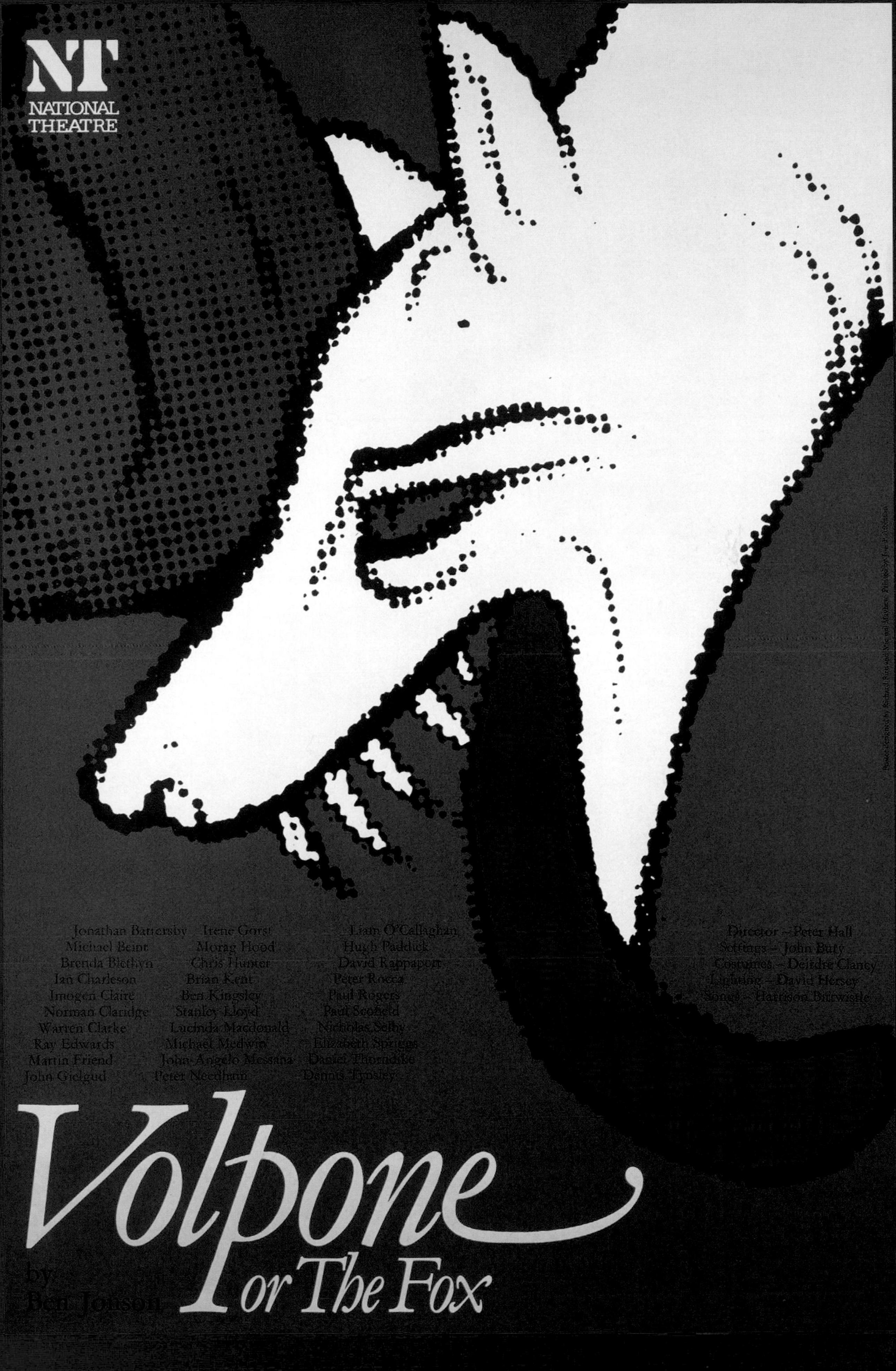

NT
NATIONAL THEATRE

THE COTTESLOE THEATRE
(small auditorium)

ALL SEATS £1.50

Timothy Block
Tony Doyle
Susan Fleetwood
Brenda Fricker
Glyn Grain
Tamara Hinchco
Louisa Livingstone
Oliver Maguire
Derek Thompson

Director Sebastian Graham-Jones
Designer William Dudley
Lighting Brian Ridley &
William Dudley

new play by
John Mackendrick

Lavender Blue

Lavender blue dilly dilly
Lavender green
I shall be king dilly dilly
You shall be queen

Not suitable for children

Poster designed by Richard Bird and Michael Mayhew. Photo by Michael Mayhew. Printed by J & P Atchison.

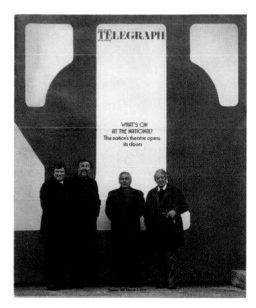

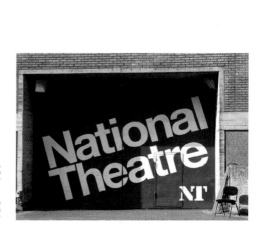

Working at Henrion's studio the new symbol for the theatre, Dennis says, came more from a feeling that 'it shouldn't be pompous, or a sans-serif, but made in the spirit of the times. The first time I saw it in use,' he adds, 'was in *The Daily Telegraph Magazine* when the theatre had opened. It was stencilled large in white on a red door.'

Michael Mayhew, the National's art director until 2009, used Dennis's design extensively, having come to the theatre as a freelance designer when it opened. 'The NT logo was great to use,' he recalls. 'Roughly square, it worked well in both landscape and portrait formats and looked good due to simple, happy shapes.' Its simplicity also meant that it could be transferred to a range of other media. 'It was used in a variety of ways,' Mayhew adds, 'projected on the building itself, or in an engraved style on glass. At different angles, or with cropping, it could be used to generate a variety of display forms.' And, in no doubt something of a personal triumph for the young designer Dennis, Briggs's celebrated poster designs of the 1970s also incorporated the logo.

To date, the NT device remains in use across the theatre's publicity material, though largely in connection with the main South Bank site, since, as the theatre's current art director Charlotte Wilkinson suggests, its design still works so well with the aesthetics of the building. 'As the theatre has grown as a global brand and expanded its audience with the National Theatre Live broadcasts in cinemas,' Wilkinson adds, 'we felt we needed to write our name in full, since the letters alone might not sufficiently convey who we are and what we do.'

The sleight of hand of the subtle combination of the N and T certainly has a resonance that would be hard to replicate. 'It has stood the test of time,' says Mayhew, 'because it is so beautifully simple, as are all the best logos.'

Edward Young
1935

Edward Young was 21 when he was dispatched to London Zoo by his employer, the publisher The Bodley Head, with orders to make sketches of penguins. In 1935, managing director Allen Lane had hit upon the idea of producing a new range of affordable but good-quality paperback books, apparently inspired by the lack of reading material available while he was waiting on the platform at Exeter station. Lane had decided on the name Penguin Books at the suggestion of his secretary Joan Coles, and when he resigned from his job in order to launch the imprint proper he required a 'dignified but flippant' symbol to go with his new venture. He asked Young to go to Regent's Park and find the penguin pool.

According to designer and writer Phil Baines, Young returned from the zoo with his drawings and the observation 'My God, how those birds stink!' But his perseverance paid off. When Lane finally brought his sixpence Penguins into the world (the company became independent of The Bodley Head in 1936), they bore a symbol that would last until 1949, when it was refined and redrawn by Jan Tschichold into something that more closely resembles the logo currently in use today.

The fact that the symbol for Lane's new publishing concept was a sea-going bird owed much to the contemporary publishing scene on the continent and, in particular, to the German reprint publishing house Albatross, which had been founded by Max Christian Wegner and John Holroyd-Reece in Hamburg in 1932. With centred text set above an elegant graphic of an albatross with its wings outstretched, the unfussy covers were designed by Hans Mardersteig, art director of the Mondadori printers in Italy, whose owner had a seat on the Albatross board.

The format of the Albatross paperback adopted the 'golden ratio' and various distinctive colourways to indicate the various genres – both techniques that were later picked up by Lane – with yellow for psychological novels and essays, orange for short stories and humorous works, and red for adventure and crime stories. Writing about the German publishers in the 1953 *Penrose Annual*, Hans Schmoller, who was then head of design at Penguin, declared that 'to this day it forms perhaps, from the point of view of design, the pinnacle among paper-covered books'.

But Schmoller had already inherited a body of design work that would set Penguin on its course as one of the world's most influential publishers in terms of what it produced and how it looked. In 1946, Tschichold arrived at Penguin and during his time there cemented the positioning of the author's name and title on the cover, cleaned up both spine and back cover layouts, and refined Young's logo (of which there were now several variants), creating eight versions of it in the process. All this was eventually enshrined in the designer's 'composition rules', which attempted to

Opposite:
Angus Hyland redesign, 2003.
—

Above:
Edward Young made many sketches of penguins at London Zoo, one of which formed the basis for the company's logo in 1935.

193 (April 1939) — first use
403 (Aug 1943) — last use ½
(also 16 on half-titles)

B1 ("Shakespeare)
April 1937 — first use

All by Edward Young

April 1939 (193) to 1943 (403)
(Mar ½ & 16 on half-titles)

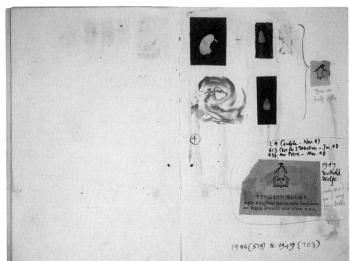

④

This on
half-title

L4 Candide — Nov. 47
613 Case for 3 Detectives — Jan. 48
633 Au Pierre — Mar. 48

1947
Berthold
Wolpe

PENGUIN BOOKS
WEST DRAYTON MIDDLESEX ENGLAND
245 FIFTH AVENUE NEW YORK U.S.A.

1946 (519) to 1949 (703)

return to J T please

please return
to J.T.
Penguin Books

J.T.'s work preparatory
to redesigning the standard
Penguin symbol

reprint

⑤ (Tschichold)

1949 (708) to 1951 (802)

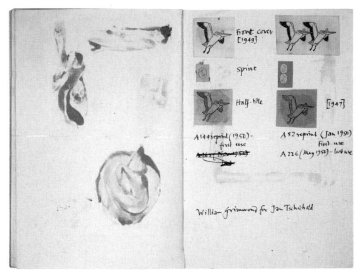

front cover
[1949]

spine

Half-title

[1947]

A144 reprint (1950) —
first use

A52 reprint (Jan 1950)
first use

A226 (May 1950) — last use

William Grimmond for Jan Tschichold

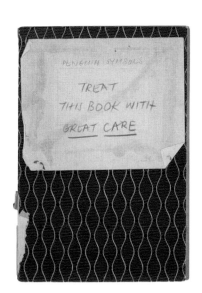

PENGUIN SYMBOLS

TREAT
THIS BOOK WITH
GREAT CARE

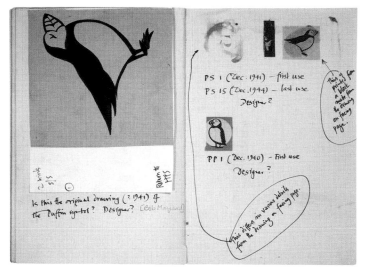

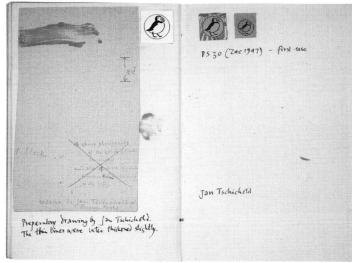

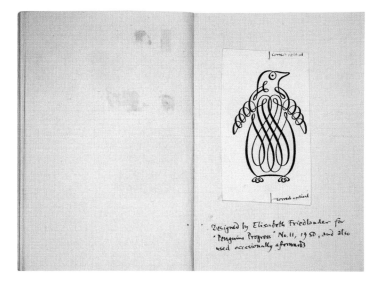

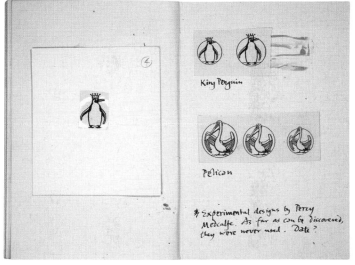

Opposite page and above:
Pages on the evolution of the Penguin
logo from Hans Schmoller's notebook
(cover shown below left).

—

Below:
Penguin logo variations over the ten
year period, 1938–48.

1938   1944   1945   1948

give Penguin's printers and typographers a unified approach to style.

'Tschichold drew the definitive penguin,' says Steve Hare, Penguin historian and secretary of the Penguin Collectors Society, 'but even that had variations – specifically in looking left or right on the book; or inside an oval; whether the oval was white or orange, etc. My understanding is that the Penguin logo should look 'into' the book – i.e., at the title, rather than turning his back on it all. So if ranged right, he should look left, and vice versa. But if ranged to the bottom of the cover, he doesn't usually look up.' As Baines revealed in his visual history of the company, *Penguin By Design*, the penguin device has gone through a host of slightly different iterations since then, and as a brand was joined along the way by other birds, most famously, the Pelican and Puffin.

The Penguin logo was extensively, though subtly, redrawn by Angus Hyland at Pentagram in London in 2003. His penguin was 15% thinner than its predecessor; it had feet that now sat on a horizon line, and a new and improved beak, neck flash and eyes. Hyland also created a series of accompanying guidelines to enable the consistent use of the symbol across Penguin's international market. Agency VentureThree has since carried Hyland's work into the digital age, creating an animated penguin ident along the way – although, famously, the penguin had been made to move in a 1980s TV campaign for British Rail, sliding down the inside of its oval border on a book cover as it relaxed into a train journey.

Young was at Penguin for just four years, and in that time contributed not only the company's inaugural penguin symbol, but also its famous banded colourways: orange for novels, green for crime and pale blue for the Pelican educational series. World War II would take him to Russia, the Mediterranean and Australia on board various Royal Navy submarines (he reached the rank of Commander), while in Germany the conflict spelled the end of the Albatross company.

In 1954, Penguin published Young's wartime memoir *One of Our Submarines* as its 1,000th paperback. The cover was designed by Young himself and encapsulates his achievements: his military honours are listed underneath his name, while the penguin logo is surrounded by a laurel wreath. It was a fitting tribute to the man who first established Penguin's distinctive and distinguished character, one which, nearly eight decades on, is recognized the world over.

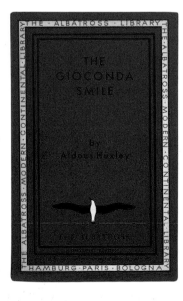

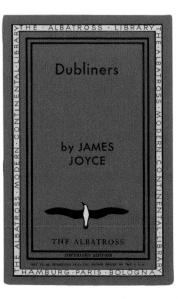

PENGUIN *Social Science* 1974-5

Anthropology/Business & Management
Economics/Politics/Psychology
Social Psychology/Sociology

Opposite:
Many covers have played with the design of the logo over the years, including this uncredited work for a catalogue of science books, *Penguin Social Science 1974–5*.

—

This page, clockwise from top left:
The cover of the second ever Penguin book, Ernest Hemingway's *A Farewell to Arms*, July 1935. It was one of the first batch of ten published and the very first 'orange' cover (number one was a blue – biography title).

—

Jan Tschichold-era book cover for Ann Bridge's *Illyrian Spring*, published in 1949.

—

David Pearson's radical 2013 cover for George Orwell's *1984*, which, in a nod to the book's theme of censorial control, blocked out the title and author's name. The book remains instantly recognisable as a Penguin.

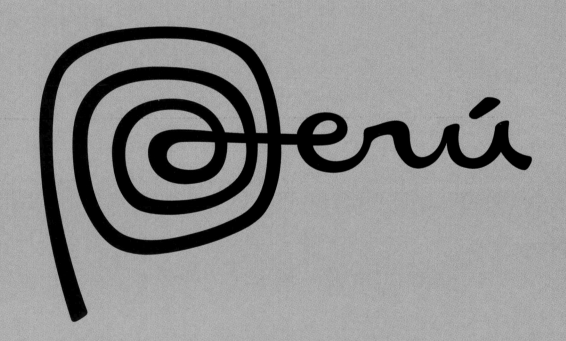

FutureBrand
Buenos Aires and Lima
2010

Designing a brand identity for a country is a challenging – some would say near impossible – task. How can a single piece of design sum up an entire nation and make reference to its wide variety of defining elements, be they geographical or historical, cultural or societal? Is there not already an insurmountable visual signifier of sorts in a national flag, familiar to both the native population and those who view the country from abroad?

But in 2010 two offices from FutureBrand South America created a logo for Peru that managed to be inclusive of the country's many diverse cultures, and evoked its long heritage and creativity, in a clever hybrid of wordmark and symbol. The result marks it out as one of the most successfully realized national identity campaigns.

A team from FutureBrand's Buenos Aires and Lima offices, consisting of staff who had previously helped to create a range of local Peruvian brands, worked on the identity at the request of PromPerú, the Peru Exports and Tourism Promotion Commission, alongside the private investment promotion agency, ProInversión. Prior to the brand development process, the team visited several towns and cities, archaeological sites, artisanal districts, museums and other institutions in different areas of the country – places linked to the three spheres that would drive the creation of the new identity: tourism, exports and investment.

'The identity is centred on the word Peru, an inclusive name which does not belong to any specific culture,' FutureBrand wrote in its brand presentation. 'Since there are many theories about its etymology, the name seems to be the product of junctions, mixtures and desires.' As the Peru brand would be serving several sectors, FutureBrand decided to forego any additional wording alongside the pronoun. 'The brand is proposed as the nucleus of a vast communicative ecosystem,' they wrote, 'which allows multiple messages, images, concepts, landscapes and cultures'. The country name was to stand alone – without the support of a directive, a message, or a neighbouring visual symbol. In fact, the single word would contain its symbol within itself, rather than use one as an extraneous device.

During the process of creating the brand, research was carried out to determine 'which were those continuous motifs to all cultures of Peru in the different regions and times,' says FutureBrand. 'The spiral form that the P has [refers] to one of the graphic motifs present in all the cultures.' According to the designers, this single letter could represent 'evolution, change, and transformation', but within the logo it also referred more directly to a fingerprint: a symbolic element in line with FutureBrand's concept that there is a 'Peru for everybody' (for 'each one'), or that it is a connection to unique discoveries. 'The use of a handwritten typography,' was about 'creating a logotype from a single line because in Peru people trace their own path based on their particular interests' says FutureBrand.

The Perú brand book created by
FutureBrand's Buenos Aires and Lima offices.

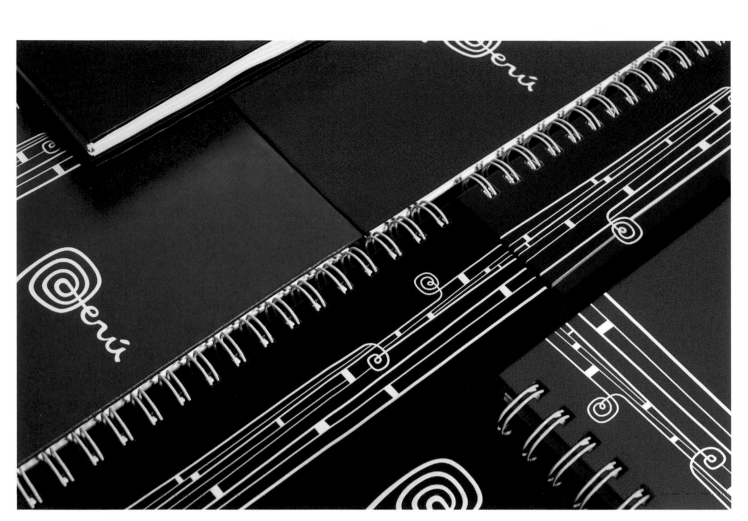

Above and below:
Additional material presenting the Perú brand, along with various colourways for logo display.
—
Opposite:
The Perú logo on a branded bag and brand book showing a close-up of the distinctive spiral.

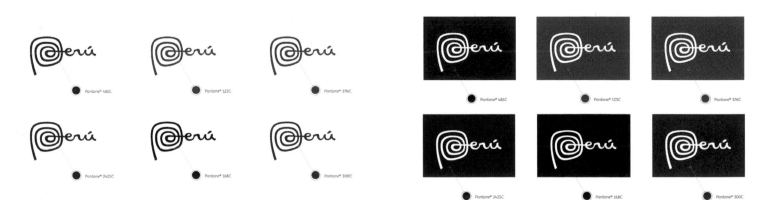

When the rubber and tyre manufacturer Pirelli first attempted to make a name for itself in America in 1908 – 36 years after being founded in Milan – a representative of the company apparently arranged for the distinctive stretched P logo to be drawn up, and the design then made its way back to Europe. Although evocative of both rubber's elasticity and the increasing speeds that were achievable with the rapidly developing automobile (and Pirelli tyres, naturally), one aspect of the identity is still something of an anomaly. Pirelli would go on to work on commercial projects with some of the most respected names in European graphic design, particularly during the 1950s and 1960s, but the name of the designer of the original and highly distinctive logotype is long forgotten.

In the late nineteenth century, Pirelli & C. had diversified from the production of telegraph cabling to bicycle tyres, and then to its first automobile tyre in 1901. In August 1907, the three-month-long Peking to Paris motor race was won by Prince Scipione Borghese, his chauffeur Ettore Guizardi and *Corriere della Sera* journalist Luigi Barzini in a seven-litre 35/45 horsepower Itala model car. That the Itala had negotiated the 9,000 mile route on Pirelli tyres – or *pneus* as they were then known – only helped to spread recognition of the name, and began an association with motorsports that would continue through the century. These early associations with the thrill of *velocità* no doubt went some way to inspire the radical treatment of the Pirelli P a year after the Itala had arrived victorious in Paris and Barzini had written up his adventures in a book.

Prior to its best-known iteration, however, the Pirelli company had many different logos in its first decades of business. 'The history of the Pirelli logo is about calligraphy rather than graphic design,' claims Pirelli's statement on the work, which describes the seemingly wilful attempts by the creators of the logo to render it differently every time. 'The elongated P initially paid tribute to the flowery and ornate taste of the time, winding around the vertical part of the letter at the expense of the loop at the top,' it continues. 'In another version [the P] wound around the word with a curving overlap into the other letters of the logo.'

In its print and poster advertising the Pirelli name was often used in conjunction with the word *pneus*, the two Ps offering plenty of opportunity for typographic play. In artist H.L. Roowy's inventive cover for the April 1914 edition of the journal *Touring Club Italiano*, the Pirelli P contains the *neu* of *pneu* and forms the radiator, bonnet and chassis of a bright-red speeding racing car. An uncredited cover of the journal from the year before had also played on the final S of *pneus*, from which a curving peloton of cyclists emerged.

According to Pirelli, the logo was finally standardized in 1945 and set in a blockier sans-serif typeface. This version then appeared on the high-quality print

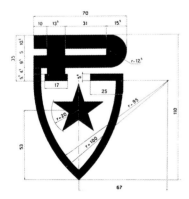

Symbol for Pirelli based on the stretched P design, 1946.

Alan Fletcher

Opposite:
Preliminary sketch for a Pirelli
advertisement by Alan Fletcher, 1959.
—
Above, left to right:
Advertisement by Pavel Michael
Engelmann, 1952.
—
Advertisement for the Cinturato
tyre by Bob Noorda, 1959.

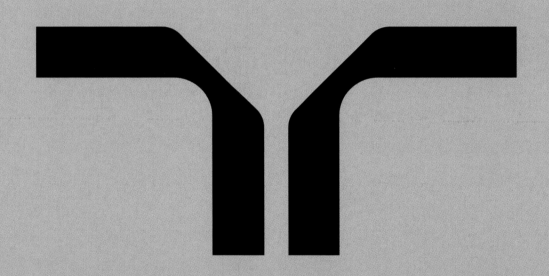

Ben Bos,
Total Design
1966

Frits Goldschmeding and Ger Daleboudt, two Dutch economics students at the Vrije Universiteit in Amsterdam, compiled their final thesis in 1960 on the subject of the increasing validity of a flexible labour market and the concept of temporary work. After graduating, the pair founded their first temporary employment agency, Uitzendbureau Amstelveen (Amstelveen Temp Office) in their home town in the North Holland province. A few years after establishing a handful of small offices in Amstelveen and Amsterdam-South, the founders changed the company name to Randstad, in honour of the industrialized area in the west of the country where, they believed, the company truly belonged. In 1966, Ben Bos of the Amsterdam studio Total Design was approached to design its logo.

'The Randstad logo story can be summarized as the outcome of my strong opinions on corporate identity,' says Bos, who joined Total in 1963, the year it was established by designers Wim Crouwel, Benno Wissing, Friso Kramer, Dick Schwarz and his brother Paul. 'I always tried to create images and design programmes that were meant to be timeless,' Bos continues. 'They had nothing to do with fashionable ideas or trends. Many of my logos survived for as long as the enterprises or institutions which they were created for did.'

RANDSTAD

Goldschmeding and Daleboudt had initially approached Dick Schwarz as an investor in their young enterprise, and the company's need for a visual identity was then brought into the Total Design studio. Schwarz approached Bos with the job because of the designer's proven record on several identity programmes. 'But I hesitated, I was not immediately enthusiastic,' Bos recalls. 'Employment services were a totally new concept in Holland, and the only established name in that kind of business was Manpower. It took a few months before I decided to have a meeting with the Randstad management. But then we came to a kind of agreement, set up a contract and I started to think about the logo.'

Bos claims he was persuaded to take on the project, despite his initial scepticism, in part because he found he would be working across all aspects of how the company presented itself. The design and appearance of Randstad's offices were to become a key part of reorganizing the business's image and, for Bos, this meant getting his hands dirty. There were to be 'clean windows, dust-free window displays and well-designed interiors,' says Bos. 'I did much of the cleaning myself, in the first year.' While even the little details, such as the flowers in the vases on the receptionists' desks, were considered, grander ambitions were also outlined with the establishment of a Randstad art collection for both public and office spaces. In addition to all these elements – a total approach if ever there was one – Bos also found time to work on the graphics for the project.

Original sketch by Ben Bos of the logo for Randstad employment agencies, 1967.

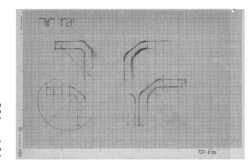

Randstad "kantoor", Randstad signage exterior.

Randstad "kantoor, personeel" signage exterior.

Randstad flagship corporate headquarters in Diemen near Amsterdam.

Randstad signage corporate interior, 2001.

Below:
Cover of Randstad USA *Design Manual*, 1995.
—

Opposite:
Randstad annual report and accompanying
'with compliments' card, 1986.

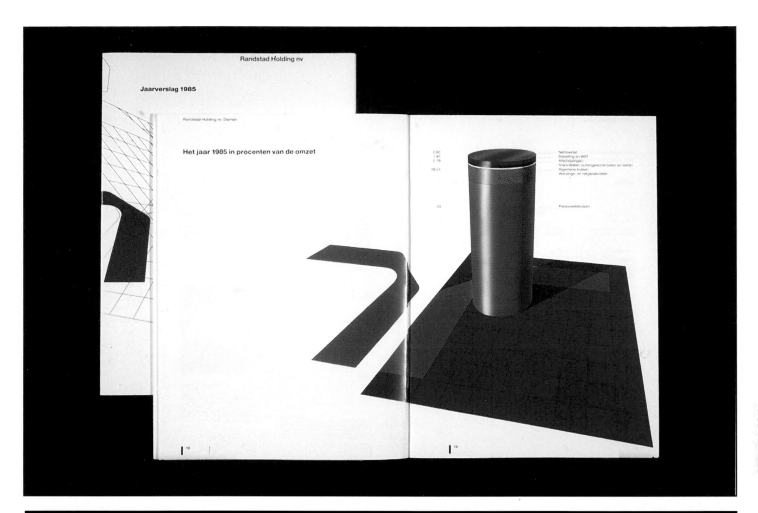

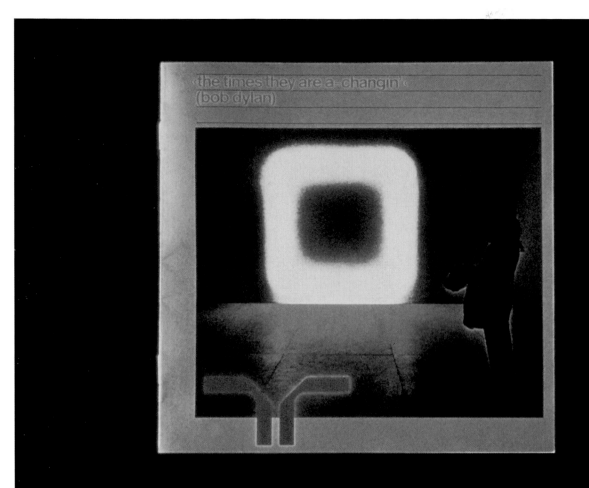

Opposite, clockwise from top:
Randstad corporate brochure, 1971.
—
Shopping bags for Randstad Staffing
Services USA, 1994.
—
Randstad paperweight, 1967.
—
Below:
Dutch poster reading 'You are at the
right place with Randstad', 1977.

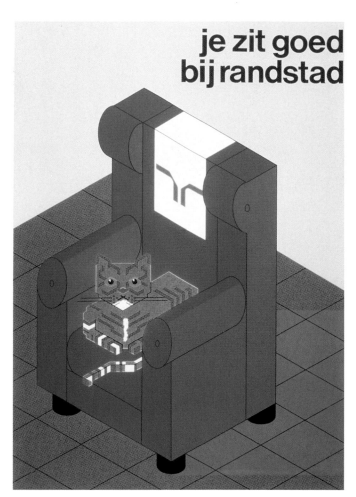

je zit goed
bij randstad

For Bos, the mid-1960s was a period in identity design 'when most logotypes were more or less abstract. Just think of Chase Manhattan Bank and suchlike. I had made a few logos myself that were kind of illustrative: a transparent typographic symbol for Alglas (1963), an importer of glass for the building industry; an abstract pile of bricks for the contractors Van Heeswijk (1967); and a colour swatch for Sukkel (1968), a firm specializing in do-it-yourself building materials. But what could I do for this new concept of finding people for employers and employers for workers?'

One of the main problems facing the designer was the fact that the products of Randstad's business were invisible. 'The firm had a rather abstract offer,' says Bos. While Manpower had borrowed the figure of the 'Vitruvian' man designed by Leonardo da Vinci, recommended by their head of marketing Jean Chanard, the industrial Randstad area had never been clearly defined, so a recognizable shape or form could not be as easily derived from this natural reference point.

Bos's solution was to turn to typography. He started by setting the initial r of the company name in lower case, as he wanted to create 'a visual image that showed a kind of efficient organization, that made a good impression on its clients, and would also have an appeal to the temporary workers who were at that time mostly female, such as secretaries and typists. So the shape of the r should have subtle, "female" details.' Having drawn a single character that he felt satisfied these criteria, Bos then realized that it would be better balanced as a symbol if it 'opened' to the left as well as the right, so he mirrored the letter.

The outcome, he says, 'meant nothing but looked fine. It was typographic without any legibility.' Moreover, it alluded to a welcoming gesture of open arms. It humanized the company, emphasizing the role that it would play in finding people work. 'It was open to the clients, open to the temp,' says Bos. 'A kind of meeting point.' Based on the r, a full alphabet was later designed by Zdena Sernets, a young Czech designer on Bos's team at Total, but the letters were only employed on minor Randstad commissions. More recently, Bos himself improved the series for an entry into a competition to use mono-space letters set up by the Dutch printers Lenoirschuring.

In 1966, Randstad had just a few offices in The Netherlands; nearly 50 years later the company is present in 38 countries, with the logo unchanged for all that time. 'My logotype survived,' says Bos. 'It has appeared on the finish line of the cycling tours in France and Spain, it is present in football stadiums and along the speed-skating rinks. And in research programs about logo recognition carried out in The Netherlands, it scored a top position.' It is, as Bos had originally hoped, working well as a timeless piece of design.

Joan Miró
1984

In 1983, in the last few months of his life and at the age of 90, the Catalan artist Joan Miró was asked if he would design a symbol for Spain's fledgling tourism industry. He agreed to the use of three elements from two pre-existing art works – a sun and star and the word *España* – and in the process helped create the first abstract symbol designed to represent a country. Miró never saw the design in use, nor accepted any payment for it, but it went on to become the most successful and recognizable national logo ever created.

Ignacio Vasallo had been made the junior minister for tourism in 1982. Vasallo's job was to help make Spain into a desirable tourist destination, a task made difficult by the fact that the country was still emerging from the shadow of the Franco dictatorship (the Generalísimo had died in 1975) and had something of an image problem. But it certainly had much to offer, and the collaborative project that Vasallo proposed to Miró helped bring millions of people to the country during the next three decades.

Vasallo developed a marketing plan that would emphasize diversity in Spain and also pay homage to its climate, which at that time was one of its principal attractions as a tourist destination. But, since 1978, central government had had no political power in the development of tourism on a national level; instead, individual regions, such as the Canary Islands or Mallorca, looked after how they appeared to the world. This was a problem for Spanish tourism in general: it had no unifying image that it could use to sell the country as a whole.

'The marketing plan was ready at the beginning of 1983,' Vasallo recalls. 'The core message was that Spain needed to position itself as "Everything Under the Sun". So I took that concept first to our in-house designers, as they had the experience, but the result was not what I wanted, it was too classical.' Vasallo's rethink involved aiming a little higher, and letters from the ministry were duly sent to three of the most famous artists in Spain at the time: Salvador Dalí, Antoni Tàpies and Joan Miró. While Vasallo met with Dalí, nothing came of it, but 'through the newspaper publisher Pedro Serra in Mallorca, who was a mutual friend of Miró and myself,' says Vasallo, 'I got a meeting with Miró at the end of the summer of 1983.'

In Mallorca, Miró was ill and conversed with Vasallo from his bed. 'I expressed what I wanted,' says Vasallo. 'I wanted an abstract sun with the word *España* on the design; everything was very clear. Miró said he was more than happy, but that he could do nothing at the moment.' Instead, the artist arranged a meeting with his dealer Francesc Farreras, and it was agreed that Miró would donate elements from two paintings he had already made to make a new design.

SOL DE MIRÓ

SPAIN by RITTS

PASSION FOR LIFE · A PERSONAL
VIEW BY HERB RITTS

'The radiance of nature, the inspiration of timeless elements. The driving forces in one's passion for life. Everything is here'

BRAVO
Spain

A 341 year old little girl.

There are things that do not age. Things that are made to be eternal. When Diego Velázquez painted "Las Meninas", he captured inmortality. Now we celebrate the 400th. anniversary of this birth. Discover his work. Could you have a better excuse to come to Spain! http://www.tourspain.es

ESPAÑA

Some of our public

beaches can be very

pri Va te

An earlier chronicler of the western Mediterranean once described the Balearics as "Islands of tranquillity not far from civilisation". And it's easy to see what he was getting at. The coastline of the islands abounds with friendly little coves, lapped by invitingly safe, blue waters. And when the siesta hour approaches it's always reassuringly possible to become the only pebble on the beach

ESPAÑA
Passion for life

Cala Agulla, Mallorca. Extensive car hire facilities are available all over the Balearics. So you can enjoy the beauty of the islands' interior as well as the seclusion of the coves

Opposite, clockwise from top:
The 'Spain By' poster campaign ran
from 1996–97 and was based on a series
of photographs from international
photographers, each focusing on an
aspect of traditional Spanish culture.
Herb Ritt's photograph shown here.
—
A poster from the 'Bravo Spain'
tourism campaign of 1998, designed
by Pedro Alonso.
—
'Passion For Life' was used as a slogan
from 1991 – 95 in a campaign by the
Spanish advertising company Delvico
Bates.
—
Below:
1986 poster making confident use of
Miro's logo alongside the original tourism
marketing slogan 'Everything Under the
Sun'.

INPROTUR · SECRETARIA GENERAL DE TURISMO · M.T.T.C.

ESPAÑA

Spain. Everything under the sun.

ESPAÑA

The letters that form the word *España* were taken from a poster that Miró had created for the World Cup in Spain in 1982; the sun and star were originally used on a poster for the Maeght Foundation in Saint-Paul de Vence that had been produced for the artist's 75th birthday in 1968. The elements were put together by Farreras, assisted by Vasallo's staff, and then approved by Miró. Vasallo was determined to pay the artist for his work but, he recalls, 'Miró said "for the King and for the government it's all free". We insisted. He said "absolutely not".'

The familiarity of the *sol de Miró* perhaps belies just how radical a proposition it was at the time. 'No-one had an abstract logo [for their country] and many people in Spain were doubtful,' says Vasallo. 'Some of the advertising agencies were unhappy, but the one we used, Tandem DDB, did good work.' That the symbol did not feature or incorporate the Spanish flag was in itself a departure from the norm. 'That was an innovation in tourism advertising, as no-one had dared to do that before,' says Vasallo. 'And it was important because it was followed, though not immediately, by many others. A few years later other countries, such as Turkey and Poland, began to use abstract logos.'

The logo was first used across Europe, then worked its way into Spanish tourism communication in the US and beyond. Although it was primarily an outward-facing design, used in campaigns to attract visitors to the country, it soon also became well known in Spain. Vasallo states that the impact on tourism was significant. In 1983, Spanish tourism generated an income of US$6.8m; by 1988 that figure had more than doubled to US$16.6m. At one point in the late 1980s, Vasallo claims, Spain was generating more income from tourism than the US.

Miró died in December 1983. His star and sun was, Vasallo says, 'probably his last gift to Spain'. It was certainly appropriate. As Spain began its journey as a democratic nation, rather than changing the country's image, the logo helped reaffirm what the country was and could be to an increasingly interested wider world.

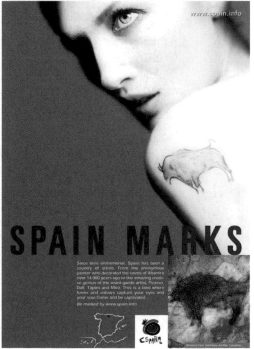

TATE

Wolff Olins
1999

The current Tate mark was designed as part of a rebrand of the entire organization in time for the launch of the Tate Modern gallery in London in 2000. The redesign of the Tate brand was undertaken as the new gallery was being built in the shell of the Bankside power station in Southwark, a couple of miles down the Thames from the original Tate Gallery, which had occupied its site in Pimlico since 1897, formerly as the National Gallery of British Art, and then becoming the Tate in 1932.

The existence of this vast new space meant that instead of continuing the location-derived names of the Tates at Millbank and Bankside, an opportunity arose to start again in the capital as Tate Britain and Tate Modern – a way to signal what kind of art people would find inside. The two other Tate sites in Liverpool (1988) and St Ives (1993) would also come under the new system.

'We needed to create something to unite all the different Tates,' says Marina Willer, who worked on the branding project as a creative director at communications agency Wolff Olins, and is now a partner at Pentagram. These days, the notion of thinking of an arts organization as a brand has become common practice, but at the turn of the millennium it was an unusual, if not controversial, idea. And Tate would soon have an identity to match.

Wolff Olins initially devised a theme to describe the brand, following a series of workshops with the Tate clients: 'look again, think again'. From there, they began to work on ideas for how this could be expressed visually. 'The way that started to translate into visuals was to think of Tate as something that is always changing, but is always Tate,' says Miller. 'Because "look again, think again" is about how art makes you constantly challenge yourself and see the world in a different way. Everyone has a different way of understanding art, it's never about being too fixed. So the whole identity had to reflect this idea of something that wasn't fixed, but was very open, very fluid.'

The final logotype, if it's even possible to call it that, is not just one mark, but a family of different logos, which move in and out of focus. 'The logos look almost exactly the same but if you look at them together, they have different intensities,' says Willer. 'So it's one way of writing Tate, which is always changing.' The variations of the Tate logo are detailed on its website. 'They range from a standard logo to a blurred version, a faded version and a halftone version (dots rather than smooth fading),' it explains. 'The marks have no fixed size or position and they are not connected with one particular Tate site. The Tate mark helps to build a brand that is fresh and fluid, but has some consistency – one Tate, with constantly changing expressions.'

The subtle variations in the family of logos evolved during the design process, which was somewhat unusual in itself. 'It wasn't created on the computer,'

The Tate logo displayed on the glass top to the Tate Modern in London.

TATE MODERN

A Bigger Splash

Painting after Performance

14 November 2012
—
1 April 2013

BOOK NOW TATE.ORG.UK
⊖ SOUTHWARK / BLACKFRIARS

FIND US ON FACEBOOK/TATEGALLERY
FOLLOW US ON TWITTER @TATE
#splash

Supported by

ART MENTOR FOUNDATION LUCERNE

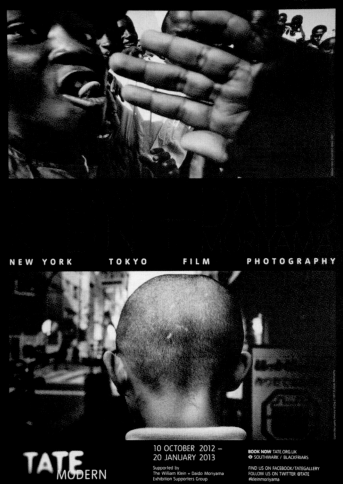

NEW YORK   TOKYO   FILM   PHOTOGRAPHY

10 OCTOBER 2012 –
20 JANUARY 2013

BOOK NOW TATE.ORG.UK
⊖ SOUTHWARK / BLACKFRIARS

Supported by
The William Klein + Daido Moriyama
Exhibition Supporters Group

FIND US ON FACEBOOK/TATEGALLERY
FOLLOW US ON TWITTER @TATE
#kleinmoriyama

TATE MODERN

Charline VON HEYL
Now or Else

LIVERPOOL TATE

ANOTHER LONDON
International Photographers Capture City Life 1930–1980

BRITAIN TATE

Opposite, clockwise from top left:
A Bigger Splash: Painting After Performance
poster by Tate Design Studio, 2012.
—
William Klein + Daido Moriyama poster
by Tate Design Studio, 2012.
—
*Another London: International
Photographers Capture City Life
1930-1980* exhibition guide booklets by
Tate Design Studio, 2012.
—
Charline von Heyl: Now or Else, Tate
Members Invitation by Tate Design Studio.
—
Below:
Pages from the Tate brand usage manual
showing the main Tate logos and logo
families, including sets for the four galleries.

says Willer. 'At the time, I was trying to find a way to make this "Tate" that was always changing. I had a little room and every day I was doing a different "Tate" and projecting it, like an installation. Then I took lots of photographs and we animated them – then did screengrabs of the animation, which became the final mark.' Not for Tate the single, definitively executed logotype. 'So they have a family of those,' says Willer, 'although they look similar, because they are different moments of the same thing.'

The Tate logotype is used across Tate Modern and Tate Britain in London, at the galleries in St Ives and Liverpool, and on all marketing and publications produced by the organization. While there are no specific rules on how the designs are used, designers would often pick a favourite and use that, says Will Gompertz, BBC art editor and former director of communications at Tate. 'A lot of designers didn't really like playing with all the different logos,' he says. 'They chose one logo and tended to stick with it.'

In its 14 years, the new Tate has grown into a significant brand, with its logo recognized around the world. The idea of Tate as a single brand hasn't always sat comfortably within the organization, however, and the various galleries – and publishing house – have expressed concern at the loss of their individual identities. The Tate's magazine, *Tate Etc.*, is an exception to the rule, having adopted its own look and logotype since replacing the *Tate Arts and Culture* publication in 2004.

But for the viewing public, the logo has appeared to make total sense, and the Tate's visitor numbers and position in the cultural world have grown significantly since 2000. 'It did create some issues within the organization,' agrees Gompertz, 'but externally it created very few.'

TATE LOGOS
CORE LOGO VARIATIONS

To communicate a brand which is constantly changing, there are five different variations of the core Tate logo. These variations should all be used at different times and in different contexts so that the full variety of logos is used, reinforcing the dynamic nature of our approach.

LOGO FAMILIES
POSITIVE LOGOS

These are the variations of the Tate logo in positive. There are five variations of the Tate core logo and four variations of each platform logo. The logos have been specially created and are available as master artworks. They should not be recreated or tampered with in any way.

V&A

Alan Fletcher, Pentagram 1989

Designed by Alan Fletcher in 1989, the logo for the Victoria & Albert Museum in London is simple yet devilishly clever. Set in the Bodoni typeface, it brings the three glyphs of the museum's nickname, V&A, together as a unified symbol, achieved by Fletcher's decision to do away with the left-hand side of the letter A and use the ampersand to reinstate the crossbar. The resulting mark is distinctive, elegant and one of the most memorable products of Fletcher's commitment to making work that produced 'a smile in the mind'.

Fletcher was working at Pentagram when he created the mark, but he was initially commissioned by the museum to create a wayfinding system, rather than a new identity. Quentin Newark was his design assistant at the time. 'Alan and I were doing a sign scheme for the V&A,' he recalls. 'It was a way of getting around the museum, which is a very complicated building. Alan had this idea of a colour representing the direction you were facing; so red was north and blue was south, etc. He had decided that the typeface would be as though it were something from the collection.'

Around the same time, the Italian publishers FMR released a facsimile edition of the original Bodoni typeface. Fletcher settled on using it for the wayfinding project and Newark redrew the font for a series of banners. 'While we were working on that the design manager at the V&A, Joe Earle, was looking to try to tidy up the V&A's identity and brand. There were a number of versions of logos.'

According to Newark, Fletcher was keen to use Bodoni because the team were starting to implement it on banner designs, but it was also an effort to reduce the number of typefaces being used by the museum. It was through experimenting with the form of the Bodoni letters that the solution came about. 'We spent a couple of weeks cutting and trying to fit and organize the letters in a beautiful way,' says Newark. 'It seems obvious now, the way that the logo's done, but I can't remember how many versions I did where we were rescaling them and changing the weights and redrawing the ampersand.'

The solution for sitting the letterforms together eventually came to Fletcher on the morning of the day the studio was presenting the ideas to the museum. 'He literally ran in fresh from the shower at home and said, "I've suddenly realized the way we should do it," and simply removed that leg of the A,' says Newark. 'The moment we did it we could see that part of the ampersand really forms the crossbar of the A, and it's all very tight and tidy.'

Newark points out that, since it was redrawn from the original version of Bodoni, the V&A logo has bracketed serifs that are not normally associated with the typeface, which more commonly has spindly slab serifs. 'The "V&A" is more authentic than pretty much all the

One of the wayfinding banners that Alan Fletcher designed for the V&A. Fletcher was working on this commission when he came up with the idea for the new logo.

Bodoni you see kicking around,' he says. 'It's a detail that's never been picked up.' The logo was implemented by the museum, replacing the array of alternative marks that had been used previously, and it has remained in use over the last two decades, and with even more prominence since the 2002 reinvigoration of the brand by Wolff Olins.

In 2010 the logo was transformed again, in perhaps its most radical way yet, at the centre of a kinetic sign created by studio Troika, the V&A Palindrome, which now hangs by the subway entrance to the museum at South Kensington Tube station. 'Inspired by the rich collection of the V&A, our aim was to create an object that would integrate theatricality and magic into the space,' says Troika's Conny Freyer. 'Very quickly we decided to work with Alan Fletcher's monogram, which lends itself to a simple yet effective typographic play whereby the letters can be twisted to deconstruct and reconnect, just like a palindrome. When Eva [Rucki] had a closer look she realized that the left stroke of the V and the right stroke of the A were two parallels, which led on to the idea that each letter could be turned around its own axis and that the logo could easily be mirrored,' Freyer continues. 'So we loved how our kinetic sign then physically exposed this logic and reinforced the magical element of seeing something for the first time.'

Newark believes that this idea would have appealed to Fletcher. 'Like any designer, he was torn between identities or logos that have a rigidity and a sameness, but also wanting it to constantly renew itself and be fresh and evolve. And the way that Troika [did that], it seems to me, is just perfect.'

Fletcher's logo achieves the knack of appearing simultaneously classical yet modern, and thus continues to be an excellent ambassador for the museum. It is also, according to Pentagram designer John Rushworth, 'a beautiful piece of observation', and it is for him this aspect that has led to its enduring appeal. 'Doing identities or creating marks is one of the things that most designers find very difficult,' says Rushworth, 'because you have to have this simplicity that in most other aspects of design you don't need. It's really a special piece of observation that Alan saw in the connection of the ampersand to the two letters. It takes a special mind to have seen that and to have honed it to that degree.'

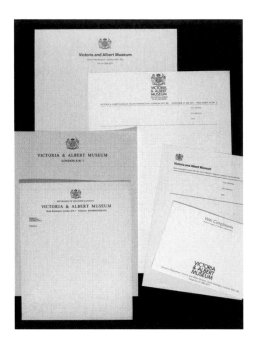

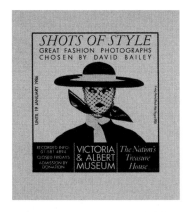

Above and opposite:
A kinetic sign designed by Troika, in which the logo spins on its own axis, is positioned by the entrance to the museum in the subway at South Kensington Tube station in London.

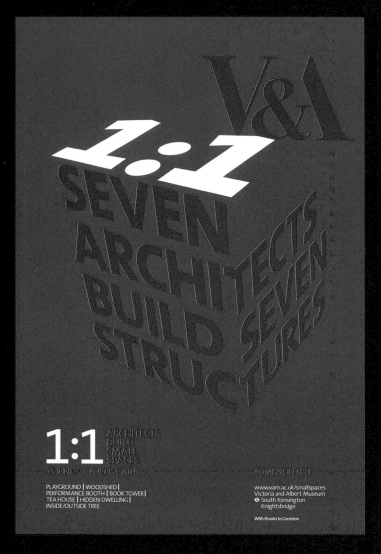

1:1

SEVEN
ARCHITECTS
BUILD
SEVEN
STRUCTURES

1:1 ARCHITECTS
BUILD
SMALL
SPACES

15 JUNE – 30 AUGUST 2010

ADMISSION FREE

PLAYGROUND | WOODSHED |
PERFORMANCE BOOTH | BOOK TOWER |
TEA HOUSE | HIDDEN DWELLING |
INSIDE/OUTSIDE TREE

www.vam.ac.uk/smallspaces
Victoria and Albert Museum
⊖ South Kensington
Knightsbridge

With thanks to Coniston

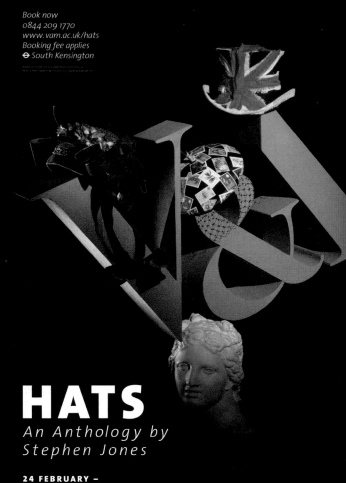

Book now
0844 209 1770
www.vam.ac.uk/hats
Booking fee applies
⊖ *South Kensington*

HATS

An Anthology by
Stephen Jones

**24 FEBRUARY –
31 MAY 2009**

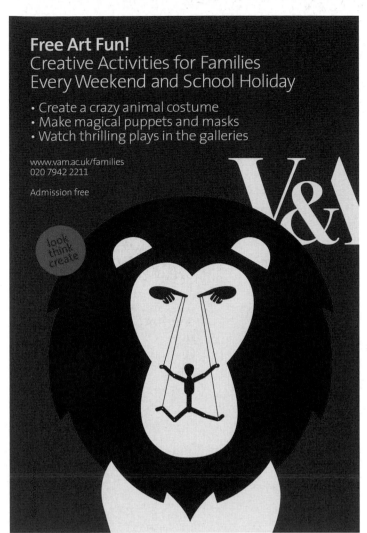

Opposite and above:
Posters for exhibitions at the V&A (2009–10)
reveal how Fletcher's symbol is often used
playfully in the museum's communications.

Franco Grignani
1964

In 1963, the International Wool Secretariat (IWS, now known as Australian Wool Innovation, or AWI), announced a design competition to create a global graphic identity for wool that would 'hold consumer confidence and represent quality standards'. The winning design – a stylized skein of wool known as the Woolmark – was launched the following year in Britain, the US, Japan, Germany, the Netherlands and Belgium.

According to the IWS of the 1960s and the modern-day AWI, the Woolmark was the work of a Milanese designer named Francesco Saroglia. His name is attached to the winning entry from the competition to design the symbol. Yet curiously for the designer of one of the most recognized logos in the world, which has been applied to over 5 billion products since 1964, nothing else is known about him. There is no record of any other work in his wider practice, no exhibitions or any projects detailed in books. How could Saroglia simply have left no trace? The simple answer is that he did not design the work at all. The logo is in fact by another, much better-known Italian designer: Franco Grignani, who died in 1999 aged 91.

There are references to the Woolmark being Grignani's work in a handful of sources. On its website, the Alliance Graphique Internationale suggests that Grignani entered the IWS competition under a pseudonym because he was part of the jury responsible for selecting the winning design. This version of events is also put forward by the designer Ken Cato in his 2007 book *Graphic Design since 1950*. Sergio Polano and Pierpaolo Vetta's *ABC of 20th Century Graphics* (2002), however, credits Grignani with the Woolmark design outright.

According to Grignani's daughter Manuela, the Alliance Graphique Internationale story approaches what really happened, but is not wholly accurate in terms of Grignani's motives. 'My father had always been a very correct man,' she says. 'He had very severe moral principles and his behaviour in the Woolmark story was inspired not by any personal profit, but by a sincere desire to represent the good standard of Italian aesthetic production.'

Grignani says that in 1964 the IWS asked her father to be a member of the international jury responsible for selecting the logo. The designer was flattered and looked forward to the opportunity to meet the other jurors in London. But before he left, Grignani says, the Italian division of the Secretariat contacted her father and asked to show him the works that were set to be entered into the competition.

'I don't think a member of a jury should see the material in a competition, but they said they just wanted to be reassured,' says Grignani. 'It's probable that they were not requiring approval, but just submitting the work to have his opinion on them. But when he saw the work my father said that the material was very poor and

WOOLMARK

According to Australian Wool Innovation, formerly the International Wool Secretariat, this image shows the hand of one Francesco Saroglia working on the Woolmark. The design is in fact by Franco Grignani.

s Isidoro **4** lunedì aprile
monday april
lundi avril

L		4	11	18	25
M		5	12	19	26
M		6	13	20	27
G		7	14	21	28
V	1	8	15	22	29
S	2	9	16	23	30
D	3	10	17	24

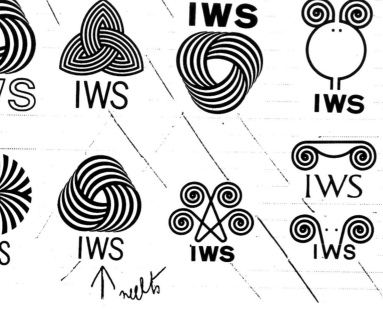

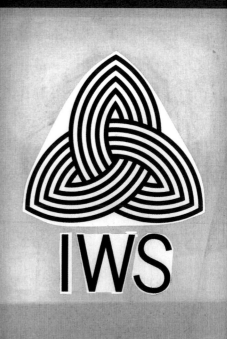

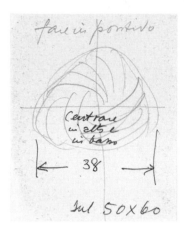

[that he] would not want to see Italy represented that way. Time was running out, they could not substitute with any other works that they had, and that is why they insisted my father should help them. And after some pressure he consented to create some logos to make their material richer.'

According to Grignani, the Italian Secretariat then decided that they would find an employee from their graphics department who could pass as the official author of the logo. 'Francesco Saroglia was a real person, an employee inside the IWS, and the collection of photographs showing him drawing the logo were obviously done after my father's logo won the competition,' says Grignani. 'It was an attempt to demonstrate the "artist" at work. The photograph of the hand painting the logo is not my father's, but Saroglia's.'

Grignani says that she in fact saw her father sketch out his ideas for the logo while at dinner. 'Being an imaginative genius, he started amusing himself trying to design a logo that could fit all the requirements,' she recalls. 'I saw my father taking a fork while dining and draw a very light scratch on the white tablecloth by means of the prongs. And it was the scratch of the actual logo: three half turns on the white tablecloth that left a thin trace on the white tissue. That evening we came home and the logo already existed. Of course, as he was so creative, he made many variants of it: thicker, thinner and so on, until he chose the right balanced variant.'

Since the competition had such a large range of international entries, Grignani may have simply presumed that he was unlikely to win. His daughter claims that during the judging process he even attempted to vote his own logo out of the competition. 'As soon as the jury started to work it was clear that his logo was the most voted,' she recalls. 'He had never suspected that and started to vote against it. Everybody kept asking him why was he voting against something beautiful that could even have been done by him. He continued to vote against it, stubbornly and desperately, out of his extreme correctness. But all of his friends, the best graphic designers, knew that he was the author and the name under which the logo competed was a fake name.'

By this point it was too late for Grignani to do anything about the work and its success in the competition. His daughter says she does not know why he felt he could not resign even the day before the judging process began, but that it was likely that he did not want to embarrass the Italian Secretariat or stir up any legal consequences for the organization. 'Sometimes in life you have to choose between two options and sometimes you choose the wrong one,' she says. 'He never thought he could win. Maybe he thought it was too late to resign, and it was incorrect to do so.'

grignani.

Soffia
la segnaletica
sui cotoni
sulle sete
La capsula
all'apogeo
capogira
sull'abisso
Gonfiano
le matematiche
sui nastri
di anni luce
Ribollono
i neutroni
nelle città
polimateriche
I sogni
con cento zeri
fan le ruote
dei motori

versi
astrusi
salvati se ben
stampati

Alfieri & Lacroix
tipolitozinco
grafia

L'uomo organizza nel vortice del suo mondo entità unificate chiamate immagini visuali. Nella grafica queste unità visive sono i segni che ci guidano nello spazio grafico. La qualità di stampa è un problema correlativo e l'emblema più prestigioso sulla bandiera dell'Alfieri & Lacroix

franco grignani

This page, top to bottom:
In Woolmark advertising the logo became
an oft-used graphic device, appearing on
woollen jumpers in this undated German
print campaign.
—
In this Spanish press ad (left) from 1988 the
Woolmark is rendered on a green on a golf
course; while in France, sheep were herded
up to form the shape of the logo (right), as
part of a 1974 campaign for wool.

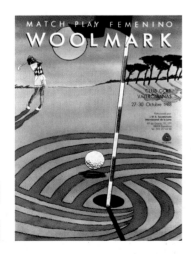

After years of what Grignani describes as 'elegant silence', it was only in the 1980s that her father officially declared that he was the designer of the logo. 'I was too young to understand his worries,' she says, 'but I know that he kept silent for so many years, swallowing bitterness any time that people attributed that superb logo to Saroglia.' But gradually Grignani went to greater lengths to put his name to the Woolmark. In 1995, at an exhibition on his work curated by Mario Piazza at Milan's Aiap Gallery, Grignani displayed a page from a diary on to which had been pasted the nine possible solutions he had entered to the IWS logo competition.

Alongside this evidence, in the wider context of his life's work, the idea that Grignani was responsible for the Woolmark makes perfect sense. His covers for *Linea Grafica* (number 6, 1965) and of *Graphis* (number 180, 1966 and the 1967–68 *Annual*), feature graphic experiments akin to the Woolmark design; the book cover for *Design aus Italien* and posters such as *Tipolitozincografia in Milano* for the Milanese printing, engraving and lithographic firm Alfieri and Lacroix show that he was playing with curved arrangements of black and white stripes in the 1960s, and furthering his interest in Op Art. In 1967 the Grignani family even sent out a New Year's card which featured a pulsating spherical graphic constructed from a series of lines.

Fellow Italian designer Massimo Vignelli has seemingly never doubted that the Woolmark is the work of Grignani. 'It is typical of his visual language,' he says. 'I never heard of any other work by Saroglia, and the fact that Grignani was on the jury justifies that he had no official entry in the competition. Saroglia may very well have been a pseudonym, or just a body, but not a real designer. If he really existed his name would be associated [with] other outstanding works in a similar language. No works; no person.'

Manuela Grignani says that her father never made any money from his Woolmark, but that 'for him it would be a great posthumous joy to see the acknowledgement of his generous talent. Now, when I meet people who knew him I always hear the same respectful words for a man who always behaved in a gentlemanly way,' she says.

'This trait of his character is fundamental to understanding his whole artistic production: graphic design, photography, paintings. He had an absolute passion for work and never felt the burden of it as it was actually a real amusement for him. 14,000 experimental works and photographs; roughly 1,200 artworks; thousands of graphic design works, covers and so on. He was an uncommon personality.'

Above and left:
Given its striking graphic qualities, the Woolmark worked particularly well at large sizes, and especially when lit up, as shown here in Piccadilly Circus in London (above), Paris (far left) and Tokyo (left), 1969–early 1970s.

Sir Peter Scott
1961

In 1986, the World Wildlife Fund (WWF) changed its name to the World Wide Fund for Nature to reflect the fact that it had moved from being a fundraising body, which collaborated with existing conservation groups, to become the world's largest non-governmental charity dedicated to the protection and restoration of wildlife habitats.

The symbol for WWF has developed alongside the new outlook, but remains true to the original version that was launched at the headquarters of the International Union for the Conservation of Nature and Natural Resources (IUCN) in Morges, Switzerland, in 1961. The black-and-white panda has since become a potent symbol for WWF's work and is indicative of its global reach.

The Morges Manifesto, signed in 1961 by 16 of the world's leading conservationists, was the organization's first call for wider financial support. 'All over the world today,' the statement began, 'vast numbers of fine and harmless wild creatures are losing their lives, or their homes, in an orgy of thoughtless and needless destruction.' Co-signatories to the declaration included Max Nicholson, the director general of the British Nature Conservancy, biologist and African wildlife expert Sir Julian Huxley and the IUCN's vice president, Sir Peter Scott, who, as a talented artist (a painter of birds in particular), would propose the symbol of a giant panda for the newly formed WWF that same year.

To design the logo, Scott refined a sketch that had been drawn by the British environmentalist and artist Gerald Watterson. Watterson's drawing was one of many he had made at an early meeting of WWF trustees, and was itself based on the image of the world's most famous panda, Chi-Chi, who had arrived at London Zoo from Beijing Zoo earlier in the year. Singling out one of Watterson's versions of the panda on all fours, facing forwards with its head angled slightly, Scott drew up a more graphic version which had much bolder contrast between the black and white patterning.

At the time, according to WWF, Scott remarked of the design that 'we wanted an animal that is beautiful, is endangered, and one loved by many people in the world for its appealing qualities. We also wanted an animal that had an impact in black and white to save money on printing costs.'

In revealing the symbol to the press at the launch of the British WWF at the Royal Society of Arts in September 1961, a carefully choreographed plan was put in place, according to Henry Nicholls, whose book, *The Way of the Panda,* charts the history of 'China's political animal'. Writing in a blog post at the time of the organization's fiftieth anniversary, Nicholls referenced a letter sent from Nicholson to Watterson regarding the programme of the launch event. 'Point six,' Nicholson wrote, 'indicates that two enlargements of the Panda logo were to be on display, one just inside the entrance and

The 2010 version of the WWF panda logo, created by Arthur Steen Horne Adamson (ASHA), allows for other imagery to appear through the design.

This page, top to bottom:
Among the attendees at the WWF Board of Trustees meetings in Morges, Switzerland in the early 1960s were Sir Peter Scott and Gerald Watterson. By November 1961 (see document on right), Scott had refined an initial panda sketch of Watterson's, a version of which appears in the document on the left.

—

The WWF panda has evolved over the years from 1961 to the present day, via Landor's redesign in 1986 (second from right). Arthur Steen Horne Adamson refreshed the identity in 2010 (far right).

Opposite:
This first official poster was so designed that it could be easily produced with the wording in any language. Designed and produced by Ogilvy & Mather, 1961.

Help to save the World's Wildlife

Your contribution
will help to save
the world's wildlife
and wild places

Send it now to:
World Wildlife Fund
2 Caxton Street
London SW1

Below and opposite:
To enable the panda design to stand for more than just a single issue, Arthur Steen Horne Adamson (ASHA) created a stencil out of the iconic symbol. This can then be used, say ASHA, as 'a window into the many different activities and environments that WWF deal with, demonstrating the breadth of WWF's work'. Clockwise from top left, these versions represent 'Climate and Energy', 'Coral Triangle', 'The Natural World', 'China Global Shift', 'Market Transformations' and 'Tigers'.

the other "on the half landing of the staircase".' The next point, he continues, revealed that 'A larger version of the Panda symbol will be displayed behind the platform. This should pose the question: why a panda at a meeting about African wildlife? At the right moment this will enable the Chairman to make the appropriate remark about the problem under discussion being a worldwide one.'

In this way, the panda became a simple visual representation of the threat to wildlife everywhere; plus, as Scott said, it resonated with the public, too. Indeed, Nicholls also wrote of how a copy of the 'appeal booklet' was sent out to key WWF members with an accompanying handout that introduced the logo. 'A Giant Panda (*Ailarpoda melanoleuca*) has been chosen to symbolize the work of the Fund,' ran the text underneath the first version of the WWF symbol, 'because it is one of the best-known and best-loved rare animals in the world, and because it owes its survival to the sort of careful conservation which all wild creatures deserve.' Interestingly, aside from spelling the genus name of the giant panda incorrectly (it should have been *Ailuropoda*), Nicholls noted that the handout's claim 'looks like pure-and-simple spin, because in 1961 the first dedicated panda reserve was still a couple of years away and the idea of panda conservation had yet to be invented.'

Yet Scott and his colleagues were able to channel this image of the rarest of animals to great effect, and it remains a thriving symbol today. 'Our iconic logo is at the heart of all our communications and used on every piece of our brand identity,' says Georgie Bridge, WWF-UK's Director of Brand Expression. 'We strive to ensure that it is always applied with respect and in its pure form.'

The shape and form of the symbol has developed over its 50 years, its most dramatic change coming in 1986 when a more balanced and streamlined version was designed by the San Francisco office of the Landor branding and design agency. Prior to the work, there were actually two versions of Scott's panda, with a more geometric design being used in the US. Design director Jerry Kuyper has said that the studio's brief was to make the panda 'not too cuddly, not too ferocious, and most certainly, not about to [become] extinct'. Writing on the *Logo Design Love* blog, Kuyper added that the team 'looked at a dozen ways to add details to the eyes before realizing the obvious – the solid black shapes were the most engaging and open to interpretation'. 1986 also saw a name change for the organization, which reflected the widening scope of its activities. The acronym WWF would remain, but it would signify the World Wide Fund for Nature.

It was in 2010 that the WWF visual identity was most radically refreshed, by branding agency Arthur Steen Horne Adamson (ASHA). The designers introduced

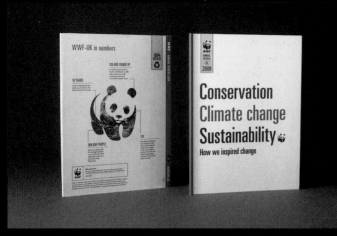

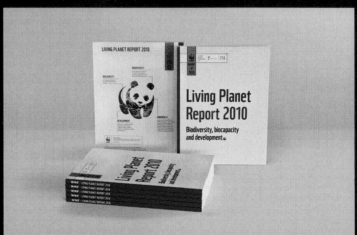

a panda stencil, which allowed a range of colour photography pertaining to a particular WWF cause to show through the parts of the symbol which would normally appear black. 'The stencil enables the iconic shape to become a lens to help express the breadth of our work,' says Bridge. Used in moving image, on the internet and, most recently, as part of an extensive iPad app, the latest version of the logo can 'really bring our work to life,' she adds, 'and let people see what's "behind the panda"'.

But the image of the panda as symbolic of the plight of the world's endangered species has not been without its critics. In 2009, the British television presenter Chris Packham argued that pandas had 'gone down an evolutionary cul-de-sac', and suggested that the vast sums of money spent on preserving them could be better spent elsewhere, not least in the protection of other species that are more significantly under threat.

But WWF certainly will not be changing its logo any time soon. 'It's a superb piece of iconic design and the equity built up over 50 years is irreplaceable', says Bridge. 'However, there is undoubtedly a challenge in ensuring that the panda is able to deliver genuine, widespread public understanding of how broad the work of WWF is in the twenty-first century. That's what we hope that the brand refresh will help achieve.'

As the statement made at Morges concluded, 'the emergency must be tackled with vigour and efficiency on the much enlarged scale which it demands ... Mankind's self-respect and mankind's inheritance on this earth will not be preserved by narrow or short-sighted means.' WWF's evocative, even emotional symbol goes some way towards embodying all those aims, and its longevity indicates its success in achieving them.

Saving tigers 🐼
Protecting biodiversity 🐼
Preserving habitats 🐼
Sustainable living 🐼

Bell System

British Rail

British Steel

CBS

Deutsche Bank

ENO

ERCO

I Love New York

NASA

National Theatre

Osborne Bull

Randstad

Sol de Miró

Tate

Centre Pompidou

Canadian National

CND

Coca-Cola

London Underground

Michelin

München 1972

Musée d'Orsay

Penguin

Perú

Pirelli

UPS

V&A

Woolmark

WWF

Index

Picture credits

4-5 © Victoria and Albert Museum, London. Design: Troika

8 © Canadian National Railway Company (CN)

10 Courtesy of the Woolmark Company

11-19 © The Estate of Saul Bass, Courtesy Jennifer Bass

20, 22, 23, 25tl, 25tr, 26 © Science and Society Picture Library

21 Courtesy Michael Johnson / Johnson-Banks

24 Photography: Alistair Hall. www.alistairhall.co.uk

25m Courtesy Cubitt Gallery

25b Photography: Laurence King Publishing

27t Image: Steve Collins. Design: British Railways Western Region, 1965

27m Image: Steve Collins. Design: British Railways Board, 1966

27b Image: Steve Collins. Design: British Railways Board 1969

28-33 Courtesy David Gentleman

34-39 CBS and the Eye Design are TM & © 2014 CBS Broadcasting Inc. All Rights Reserved.

40 © Centre Pompidou, Paris, France, Design: Jean Widmer, 1977

41-42, 43t, 44-47 Courtesy Jean Widmer

44b Photography: Georges Meguerditichian - © Centre Pompidou, 2013

48, 52 © Canadian National Railway Company (CN)

49 © Canadian National Railway Company (CN). Source: Library and Archives Canada/Allan Fleming/C-110428

50t © Canadian National Railway Company (CN). York University's Clara Thomas Archives & Special Collections (ASC) / Toronto Telegram Fonds F0433

50b, 51t, 53bl, 53br © Canadian National Railway Company (CN). York University's Clara Thomas Archives & Special Collections (ASC) / Allan Fleming Fonds F0529

51b © Canadian National Railway Company (CN). York University's Clara Thomas Archives & Special Collections (ASC) / Allan Fleming Fonds F0529. Photography: Kryn Taconis, 1962

53t © Canadian National Railway Company (CN). Source: Library and Archives Canada/James Valkus/C-110429

53tm © Canadian National Railway Company (CN). Source: Library and Archives Canada/Allan Fleming/C-136035

53lm © Canadian National Railway Company (CN). Source: Library and Archives Canada/Allan Fleming/C-136034

54 Courtesy Campaign for Nuclear Disarmament (CND) Archives. Design: Ken Garland. Origination of symbol: Gerald Holtom

55-57, 58t, 59t Courtesy Campaign for Nuclear Disarmament (CND) Archives

58b © CND Cymru

59m Courtesy Campaign for Nuclear Disarmament (CND) Archives. Photography: Ben Soffa

59b Courtesy Campaign for Nuclear Disarmament (CND) Archives. Photography: Sue Longbottom

60-67 Courtesy of The Coca-Cola Company

68-71, 73 Courtesy Deutsche Bank

72 © Stankowski-Stiftung

74 © ENO / Design: Mike Dempsey / Carroll, Dempsey & Thirkell

75 Courtesy Mike Dempsey

76tl Design and art direction: Mike Dempsey. Photography: Holly Warburton. Design Group, Carroll, Dempsey & Thirkell

76tm Art direction: Mike Dempsey. Design Barbro Ohlson. Illustration: Dirk Van Doren. Design Group, Carroll, Dempsey & Thirkell

76tr Design: Fernando Gutiérrez. Art direction: Mike Dempsey. Photography: Holly Warburton. Design Group, Carroll, Dempsey & Thirkell

76br Design and art direction: Mike Dempsey. Photography: Tony Evans. Painting detail from *L'Amour et Psyché* by François-Edouard Picot

76bm Art direction: Mike Dempsey. Design: Fernando Gutiérrez. Photography: Robert Shackleton

76bl Design: Mike Dempsey.

77l Design: Mike Dempsey. Photography: Michael Hoppen.

77tr Art direction: Mike Dempsey. Design: Barbro Ohlson. Photography: Uri Weber

77bl Art direction: Mike Dempsey. Design and illustration: Iain Crockart

78 Courtesy Mike Dempsey

79 Art Direction: Mike Dempsey. Design: Fernando Gutiérrez. Design Group Carroll, Dempsey & Thirkell

80 Design and art direction: Mike Dempsey. Photography (top) Barbra & Zaffa Baran (bottom) Lewis Mulatero. Design Group, Carroll, Dempsey & Thirkell.

81t Truck design and copywriting: Mike Dempsey. Design Group, Carroll, Dempsey & Thirkell.

81m, 81b Design, art direction and photography: Mike Dempsey. Design Group Carroll, Dempsey & Thirkell

82-89 © ERCO

90, 92, 93m, 93b © New York State Department of Economic Development (NYSDED). I♥NY and I LOVE NEW YORK are trademarks and service marks of New York State Department of Economic Development used herein with permission.

91, 93t © New York State Department of Economic Development (NYSDED). Digital image, The Museum of Modern Art, New York/Scala, Florence

94-95 Courtesy Milton Glaser Studio

96-100, 101tl, 101tm, 101b, 103t, 103m © TFL from the London Transport Museum collection

101tr © TFL from the London Transport Museum collection and Estate of Abram Games

102l © Transport for London. Peter McDonald, *London Underground Party*, 2008. Commissioned by Art on the Underground as part of *100 Years, 100 Artists, 100 Works of Art*

102r © Transport for London. Lothar Götz, *Visions of a Roundel*, 2008. Commissioned by Art on the Underground as part of *100 Years, 100 Artists, 100 Works of Art*

103b © TFL / Agency: M&C Saatchi / Creative team: Joe Miller and Tristan Cornelius / Illustration: Tokyo Plastic (Picasso)

104-109 © 2014 Michelin. All rights reserved.

110-112, 115 Prof. Coordt von Mannstein und die Gesellschafter des "Graphicteam" Hans Buschfeld, Winfried Holz, Heinz Lippert, Siegfried Himmer. Erscheinungsbild der Olympischen Spiele 1972: Ottl Aicher. Photography: von Mannstein.

Acknowledgements

This book has been a collaborative effort from start to finish. My thanks go to my colleagues and friends at *Creative Review* who, in March 2011, worked on putting a special issue of the magazine together all about logos. This book therefore contains research and writing by Patrick Burgoyne, Gavin Lucas and Eliza Williams.

At Laurence King I would like to thank Sophie Drysdale and Sarah Batten for helping to get the project off the ground. I am also especially grateful to my editor, John Parton, for seeing the book through and for keeping everything ticking over (particularly me). A special thanks also to Mari West who has done a great job sourcing the images and to Nathan Gale of Intercity for sewing everything together on the page.

Collaborations really began when we researched the logos issue at CR, with valuable input coming from our readers and from a host of designers and experts who we consulted – in particular, Marina Willer, John Bateson and Angus Hyland. This starting point then gave me the opportunity to build up a more extensive collection of some of the very best examples logo design has to offer.

I would also like to thank Gerry Barney, Ben Bos, Richard Danne, Mike Dempsey, Ian Dennis, Michael Evamy, Martha Fleming, Justine Fletcher, David Gentleman, Paul Giambarba, Daniela Grignani, Manuela Grignani, Steve Hare, Lewis Laney, Coordt von Mannstein, Professor Ian McLaren, Bruno Monguzzi, Mark Ovenden, David Pearson, Paul Pensom, Anna Richardson-Taylor, Alessandro Rinaudo, Ted Ryan, Adrian Shaughnessy, Ignacio Vasallo, and Jean Widmer.

Finally, this book is for my girls – Iris, Rose and Emma.

Designers and experts who offered opinion on their favourite logos were: Marksteen Adamson; David Airey; Philippe Apeloig; John Bateson; Michael Bierut; Connie Birdsall; Tony Brook; Mike Dempsey; Michael Evamy; Bill Gardner; Bryony Gomez-Palacio; Sagi Haviv; Angus Hyland; Michael Johnson; Peter Knapp; John Lloyd; Miles Newlyn; Paula Scher; Tony Spaeth; Armin Vit; Marina Willer; Michael Wolff.

LAURENCE KING

Published in 2014 by
Laurence King Publishing Ltd
361–363 City Road, London,
EC1V 1LR, United Kingdom
T +44 (0)20 7841 6900
F + 44 (0)20 7841 6910
—
enquiries@laurenceking.com
www.laurenceking.com
—
Text © 2014 Mark Sinclair
Mark Sinclair has asserted his right under
the Copyright, Designs, and Patents Act 1988
to be identified as the author of this work.
—
This book was produced by Laurence King
Publishing Ltd, London
—
A catalogue record for this book is available
from the British Library
—
ISBN: 978 1 78067 165 9
—
Design: Intercity
www.intercitystudio.com
—
Printed in China